Me and Ernie

Growing Up on Baseball in the Sixties and Finally Celebrating A Cubs World Series Title

Timm Boyle

FOREWORD FROM THREE-TIME WORLD SERIES CHAMPION BOBBY RICHARDSON

Disclaimer

The events that occur in this book are true, recounted from the best of my memory. I've reconstructed dialogue from memory, which means that it may not be word for word. But the essence of what was done and said is accurate. I have changed the names of friends, acquaintances and anyone else who is not a public figure in order to protect their privacy. My family's names are real.

Acknowledgments

Thanks to Kristin Finaldi for the cover design, family members for proofreading the manuscript, and baseball fans for buying the book.

Cover photo credit: Chicago Baseball Museum

Dedication

To the one and only… Ernie Banks

Table of Contents

Foreword by

Bobby Richardson

I met William Boyle, Timm's dad, many years ago when he worked for Moody Bible Institute. Bill knew as much about two subjects – the Bible and baseball – as anybody I'd ever met. Timm was very fortunate to have Bill as his father, and it's obvious from this memoir that he is fully aware of that.

Although I did not grow up as a Cubs fan, I'm sure I would have been one if I'd been raised in the Chicago area as Timm was. I still remember those visits to the Boyles' home in Oak Park, Illinois following Saturday afternoon Yankees-White Sox games at Comiskey Park in the Sixties. I enjoyed the family's hospitality, and it was wonderful talking baseball with Bill, his wife, Jeanne, and their kids.

Many years have passed since then, and it's hard to believe that entering the 2016 season the Cubs had not won a World Series in 108 years. Fortunately, that streak finally came to an end, and I know Timm and many other long-suffering Cubs fans are celebrating it enthusiastically.

During my playing days, I was blessed to be a member of a team that was very familiar with the World Series. In fact, the New York Yankees won the American League pennant nine times during my 12-year career. We captured the World Series title on four of those occasions, and I played in three of them so I know first-hand how much joy comes from a Fall Classic victory.

I'm very happy that Chicago Cubs fans now know what it feels like to be on top of the baseball world. And considering how young, deep and talented this current Cubs team is, I wouldn't be surprised to see them back in the World Series again very soon.

In the spring of 2016, I said, "It's going to happen someday for the Cubs!" I'm glad "someday" arrived just a few months later.

On Deck

Introduction

The Chicago Cubs are the World Champions of baseball! (Just in case you hadn't heard.)

For decades I wondered if I was ever going to be able to say those words. But now I can. And as much as I'd love to see the Cubs repeat in 2017, I'm hoping for a long off-season in order to bask in the glow.

When the 2016 season began, I made the embarrassing confession that I was a lifelong fan of a baseball team that had not won a World Series in 108 years.

Yeah, there were a few times during my 63 years on Earth when I tried to stray from the allegiance I felt for the Chicago Cubs. I even thought about becoming a White Sox fan once or twice, and there were a couple of occasions when I pretended not to care. But then the Cubs would go and win a game and I'd be right back in the same disgusting relationship.

A hopeless feeling overcame many Cubs fans during the latter part of the 20th century and the first 15 years of the 21st century. It was ingrained in us following decades of frustration and failure. And as far as the Cubs winning a World Series during my lifetime was concerned… well, let's just say I was a tad skeptical, even during the 2016 season when they appeared to have as good of a shot at it as anybody.

It's not like I had nothing else to do through the years other than lament the fact that my team was closely associated with "lovable losers." But even with plenty else to occupy my heart and time –

including a wonderful family and a great job – I continued to tune into Cubs games as often as I could, watched highlights on the local newscasts and ESPN's SportsCenter, read online stories for more details, and occasionally made it out to Wrigley Field for a game. I still felt a pang of sorrow when the Cubs lost and a sense of pride when they won. I understood very well that this was a sickness, and I certainly wasn't proud of it.

I also knew I wasn't alone. I guess misery really does love company because there are millions of Cubs fans out there, including many who suffered as long or longer than I did. They were just as sick as I was. We were all a bunch of codependents, living and dying with the fortunes of a team that could never win it all. We got too excited when they did well and made too many excuses when they didn't. Unconditional love? Nah, just plain stupid.

So, why did I write this book? The original purpose was not to examine how a team could avoid winning a World Series for well over 100 years because that would have been far too difficult.

Actually, I wrote this memoir for two reasons. First, I wanted to chronicle my longtime relationship with baseball in general and the Cubs in particular in order to come to some kind of understanding regarding why I continued to hold out hope for a ball club that had broken so many records for ineptitude and so many hearts with disappointment.

Second, and this is intricately intertwined with the first, I wanted to explore the reasons behind how it's possible to be so bad for so long and yet be so loved. Because once that "Prodigal Son" concept is grasped, I think it becomes feasible for me to comprehend how God could love someone like me. And you. And maybe even the Cubs.

Fortunately, all that stuff is overshadowed by one simple fact: the Chicago Cubs are the World Champions of baseball! (Just in case you hadn't heard.)

First Inning

Field of Screams

I wish I could recall my first-ever visit to Wrigley Field, but the memory is as faded as a 1945 Cubs World Series pennant.

These days, when I approach this incredible shrine to baseball, I often forget to be awed. Familiarity breeds contempt, I suppose. But I'm making a promise to myself as I write these words that next time I visit this historic ballpark on Chicago's north side, I'm going to do it in complete silence. I'll allow all my eager senses to ravenously absorb every piece of breathtaking data and process it with the open and vulnerable mind of a child filled with wonderment at what lies before him.

I'll listen attentively as vendors hawk their various wares along Addison Street. My ears will be tuned to the cryptic, "Who needs two?" muttered by scalpers avoiding eye contact on Sheffield Avenue and the shouted greetings from people meeting friends at prearranged destinations along bar-lined Clark Street.

The shuffling of feet and the metallic grinding of the turnstiles will be a symphony to my ears as I enter the beloved ball yard, while the crack of the bat and the smack of leather will penetrate my eardrums and spark memories of times long past when baseball was truly an American institution and the most popular sport in the country.

I'll firmly grasp the cool-to-the-touch, rounded railings separating sections of seats in the boxes and grandstands, run my hands across the plastic seat backs as I stride along the cement walkway, and tilt my head back to feel the Lake Michigan breeze rushing to greet my face. I'll breathe in deeply to fully capture the ever-present smells emanating from hot dogs, brats and nachos, and I'll eat and drink

3

slowly to allow my tongue to fully savor the tastes of salted peanuts and cold beverages.

I'll gaze intently at the deep green grass in the outfield and infield, the thick green ivy lining the outfield walls, and the huge green hand-operated scoreboard in center field. The rich brown infield dirt, the solid blue Cubs caps with the red "C" worn by fans and players alike, and the bright yellow numbers marking the distance from home plate to the outfield wall will create a rainbow of joy for my adoring eyes.

Finally, I'll closely examine the weathered faces of men and women, and the innocent visages of boys and girls, as they smile, grimace, laugh, sigh, sing, shout and thoroughly enjoy one of the most extraordinary and rewarding experiences this side of Heaven.

* * *

It's my older brother's fault, for crying out loud. He's not a Chicago Cubs fan anymore, but he was a diehard fan who bled Cubbie blue in the 1950s and 1960s. Because I mimicked everything he did and said during my formative years, I became a Cubs fan, too.

I was six years younger than Bill (still am), and if he had told me to go play in traffic as a kid, I'm sure I would have obeyed with no questions asked. In fact, I probably would have thanked him for the opportunity to improve my dexterity by dodging oncoming vehicles.

I idolized Bill. He was everything I wanted to be – older, taller, smarter, more popular – and so I wore my baseball cap just like him, tried to talk like him, chewed gum like him, spit like him (mostly outdoors), oiled my baseball mitt like him and stuck a ball in the pocket of my infielder's glove and wrapped a thick rubber band around it for the winter like him. Just like Bill, I opened my baseball card packs from top to bottom instead of across the top and placed duplicate cards of marginal players in the spokes of my blue Schwinn bike to make it

4

sound like a roaring motorcycle.

How did Bill show his appreciation for my meticulous imitation and unbridled adulation? By treating me like just about everybody treated their smaller siblings back in the day, regardless of the hero worship engaged in by the younger – never missing an opportunity to make me feel like the lowest piece of scum on the planet. He made fun of me for my pointed right ear, my shiny nose and my general incompetence at everything I attempted to do. (I'm really glad I didn't contract polio as a kid, or perhaps my limp would have become fodder for humor as well.)

My older brother was relentless. Even when our father would silence him at the dinner table, Bill would patiently wait until our parents' faces were in their plates, gain my attention by nudging me under the table with his foot, then point to his ear or nose and give me that sick smirk, as if saying, "Not only are you an absolutely worthless, stupid little twerp, you're ugly, too." I'd scream and he'd play innocent, and Mom and Dad would shake their heads and wonder what they did to deserve two such imbeciles.

I grew up in rather urban Oak Park, Illinois – living there for the first eight years of my life – and with the exception of a few daring ventures to parks with actual grass, we played almost all our sports in the rugged alley behind our house on Home Avenue. As a young, puny kid, it seemed like an adequate place to play, but I went back there a number of years ago and was amazed to discover that the alley is only seven inches wide.

OK, ya nitpicker, it's somewhat larger than that, but not much. That beloved alley with its Exxon-sized oil stains, jagged cracks and Grand Canyon-like holes served as a softball diamond in the spring and summer, a football field in the fall, a hockey rink in the winter and a basketball court year-round.

During baseball season, the 16-inch softball would fly off the bats of the big kids and frequently wind up in somebody's backyard after rattling off a house, garage, swing set, fence or an unfortunate cat. Not to worry. The Dawson's yard was an automatic double, the Miller's a triple, the Rutherford's a fly out, etc. Launching one into our yard, down at one end of the block and closely guarded by our faithful dog, Skippy, would have counted as a home run. But nobody ever hit it that far, for which my parents were grateful.

Being a pint-sized kid, I rarely hit the ball at all, despite the fact that a 16-inch softball seemed as large as a beach ball as it floated toward me from the underhanded toss of a neighbor. With the exception of one other kid on our block – Danny Kitner – everybody was at least four years older than I was. The only reason Danny and I were allowed to play was because our dads insisted that the older kids allow us to.

That kind of stuff wouldn't work these days. If a parent today told adolescents to let another little kid play in their game, first they'd tell the adult where to go, then they'd come back at night and spray paint the guy's garage with gang slogans or threaten to kill him if he ever spoke to them again. But back in the Fifties and Sixties, kids actually had respect for authority, and they did what they were told by adults even if they didn't like it.

I'm pretty sure that's when the older kids started hating me. Danny and I would be the last ones picked every time, with Danny relegated to one team that didn't want him and I reluctantly accepted by the other. They would invariably stick us in right field where we could do the least amount of damage, but eventually we'd have to come to bat. That's when Bill and the other older kids would incessantly remind me how much I sucked.

Of course, we didn't say "suck" in the Fifties. It was more like, "You tool! Come on, Junior Keen. Hit the ball for once in your pathetic life!" Not exactly Eminem material, but it still felt lousy hearing that stuff every day, especially from an older brother whom I revered. I always hoped Danny and I would be placed on the same team against

6

the bigger guys because I was much more interested in going through a game – or an inning, for that matter – without getting yelled at than I was in winning.

But there were a couple of things I accomplished in that death valley of an alley that actually impressed the neo-Nazis on our block. One was my willingness to slide during games of Running Bases. Two older guys would play catch, one at one base (a lengthy crack in the cement) and the other at another base (a second crack), about 10-15 yards apart. Anytime one of them dropped the ball or overthrew the other, the runners would take off and see how many bases they could run, back and forth, before stopping safely at a base or being tagged out.

I discerned from watching baseball on television that on close plays, sliding runners had an advantage over those who approached a base standing up. So, I'd build a pile of soft, moist leaves near each base to cushion the contact with my butt, and I'd slide whenever necessary to avoid being tagged. The bigger kids thought I was crazy, but I noticed a spark of admiration in their eyes after I recklessly subjected my body to the pavement, and I thrived on that.

The other was a one-time event. We were playing touch football one Saturday morning and I went out for a pass with brother Bill "defending" me. He knew there was no way that Ronnie Miller the quarterback was going to pass the ball to a 6-year-old punk like me, so he left his post and rushed the QB (after the obligatory, quick three-count). I also was well aware that Miller wasn't going to select me among his receivers, even if nobody was covering me, but I stuck my arms out anyway, as I was repeatedly ordered to do.

Well, Miller must have experienced a brain cramp when my brother frazzled him with his surprise rush because he lofted the pigskin in my direction. To this day, I have absolutely no idea how I caught that football. I never even turned my head to see if it was coming my way. All of a sudden it was in my hands and I was running toward the goal line. This was unbelievable. It shocked everybody in the alley that day,

7

and I'm pretty sure time momentarily stopped, much like in the movie *The Day the Earth Stood Still.*

Now viewing this surreal scene from a distance of about 20 to 30 yards, did my brother choose to let me score the first – and undoubtedly last – touchdown of my Oak Park alley career? No chance. Bill was the ultimate competitor, and there was no way he was going to let a scrawny little runt of a brother burn him for a TD. He raced after me, covering 10 yards for every five of mine, and caught me a few yards shy of the goal line with a two-handed tag that constituted a tackle in our game.

It's funny, but I didn't really care that I hadn't scored. Just to see the astonished looks of my older teammates and to be patted on the back and have my hair mussed up in the huddle – as Wally Cleaver would playfully do with the Beave now and then – was worth it all. Bill and his teammates quickly made it clear that I was the "luckiest scab who ever lived," but nothing was going to wipe the silly grin off my face after that play. I relived that event in my mind repeatedly for weeks, and the fact that it's still a vivid memory today tells you something, although I'm not sure what.

I mentioned Bill's competitive nature. He doesn't exhibit it as much today, but back when he was younger it was really something to behold. When he was a sophomore or junior in high school and I was about 10 or 11, we would play that indoor hockey game with the players who "skated" up and down the "ice" when you pushed, pulled and twisted the knobs at your end of the game. The oversized puck was bulky and slow – and approximately 10 times the size of a player's head – so we used a small marble instead. The action would get fast and furious.

We played a full season of games with the original six National Hockey League teams – Boston Bruins, Chicago Blackhawks, Detroit Red Wings, Montreal Canadiens, New York Rangers and Toronto Maple Leafs – and Bill would use his track stopwatch to keep tabs on our two-minute periods, stopping the watch each time somebody scored or the marble went sailing over the sideboards and whizzing by one of our heads.

Sixteen-year-olds are generally more skilled than 10-year-olds when it comes to hand-eye coordination games, and while that was also definitely the case with us, we were pretty even in the won-loss department due to the fact that when Bill would lose his temper, his concentration would slip away. Plus, I was really lucky.

A typical game would feature Bill applying incredible pressure with vicious slap shot after slap shot and wicked wrist shot after wrist shot, but somehow my goalie would make one amazing save after another. Then, out of desperation, my defenseman would fire the marble out of my defensive zone. Sometimes it would bounce against the boards, ricochet off several players from both teams and miraculously deflect into his net for a goal.

This would cause Bill to shout "No!" at the top of his lungs – after lunging to stop his stopwatch – and call me the luckiest little squirt in the world. I'm not sure if I've ever told him this, but on days when I didn't wish to raise his ire, I'd actually let Bill win. Imagine that. I was a 10-year-old taking a dive in a game against my 16-year-old brother so that he'd feel better about himself and so my self-esteem wouldn't plummet any farther. Yeah, that's pretty healthy.

But Bill didn't spend all his free time hollering at me. In fact, he dedicated a vast majority of the time we spent together to teaching me everything about sports that it's possible for a little kid to know. He made sure I knew all the rules to every sport and all the names of the key players.

He also spent countless hours improving my fielding and throwing by hitting grounders and fly balls to me on the huge grass field in front of the Wheaton College gymnasium after we moved from Oak Park when I was eight. And every time I told him I was too tired to

9

keep playing, he'd make a comment comparing my glove or arm to a big league star, and that would give me the incentive to keep going.

He'd protect me crossing the street. He'd come to my aid if I was getting picked on by a bigger kid. He'd take me to Cubs and White Sox games. He'd make sure I didn't get ripped off in baseball card trades with older kids. Bill did all the great stuff you'd want an older brother to do. And decades later, he'd do the same types of things if I ever needed him to.

Second Inning

Up Close and Personal

My favorite athlete growing up, bar none, was Ernie Banks. Nineteen-fifty-three was not only the year I was born, but also the year Ernie made his major league debut. Coincidence? I think not.

I've always felt a certain affinity toward Ernie. What am I talking about? I practically worshipped the guy. Sitting in the left field bleachers for his 500th career home run is still the biggest in-person sports thrill of my life. (More later on that incredible moment and how I got in trouble for witnessing it.)

The first time I heard Ernie make one of his annual, rhyming, preseason predictions, I think I was six years old. It was something along the lines of, "The Cubs will be fine in 1959."

"Really?!?!" I exclaimed aloud, my eyes as wide open as Opie Taylor's after catching a fish with the new pole Andy bought him for Christmas. "Will the team that finished 20 games out of first place in the National League last year actually be fun to watch this season? Will the Cubs win enough times to maybe contend for the pennant?"

I ran to my dad with the glorious news. But he just shook his head, gave my noggin a gentle rub and said, "Ernie says that type of thing every year, son. It doesn't mean anything. The Cubs will be mediocre at best."

Ouch! That was easy for my dad to say. He was never a Cubs fan. He grew up in the Philadelphia area and as a kid cheered on the powerful Athletics as they won a number of American League pennants and World Series with the likes of Lefty Grove, Al Simmons, Jimmie Foxx, Mickey Cochrane and my dad's personal favorite, second

11

baseman Max Bishop. Dad became a Philadelphia Phillies fan when the A's moved to Kansas City in 1955, and eventually landed a business job in the Phillies organization.

My father was a second baseman when he played ball, and that's what he wanted me to be. He'd station me at that position whenever we played ball together with my brothers and neighbors. And he'd tell my Little League coach at the beginning of each season that it was a waste of time to put me anywhere else. I would occasionally play other infield positions such as shortstop, and sometimes I'd fill in as an outfielder, but I always wound up back at second base.

I guess it's not surprising that my dad's favorite player during the 1960s was another second baseman. Bobby Richardson, who Dad had met at some point, was the epitome of the man my father wanted me to become someday. A heavy-duty Christian with a slight frame, Richardson was better known for his great glove than for his stick, especially when he first came up to the majors.

Bobby made his living with his mitt, garnering five consecutive Gold Glove awards, and he learned to hit better as his career progressed. In fact, he batted over .300 in both 1959 and 1962, leading the American League in hits with 209 that latter season. But nowhere was he as impressive with the hickory as when the bright media glare would shine on the World Series.

There were two things nobody would have guessed heading into the 1960 Fall Classic. One was that the Yankees would outscore the Pittsburgh Pirates by 28 runs but lose the Series. The other was that with Mickey Mantle, Roger Maris, Yogi Berra, Whitey Ford, Bill Terry, Bob Turley, Moose Skowron and Clete Boyer all performing for the Yankees, Richardson would be awarded the Series MVP. But both miraculously occurred. To this day, Richardson remains the only player from a losing team to claim the World Series MVP award.

The second sacker was a lifetime .266 hitter, and he batted .252

12

with only one home run and 26 RBI in 1960. But Bobby smacked a grand slam and drove in a Series single game-record six runs in Game Three of the 1960 Fall Classic. He then legged out two triples in Game Six, winding up with a Series-record 12 RBI, 11 hits and a .367 batting average.

Although he hit .261 in 1961, Richardson excelled in the postseason again, batting .391 with a Series-high nine hits in the Yankees' four games-to-one triumph over the Cincinnati Reds.

In Game Seven of the 1962 World Series, it was Richardson who snared a vicious line drive by Willie McCovey with two outs in the bottom of the ninth inning – with the potential tying and winning runs in scoring position – to preserve a 1-0 win and the Yankees' World Championship over the San Francisco Giants. Two years later, Bobby was at it again, following up a .267 campaign with a Series-best 13 hits and a .406 batting average that included a pair of doubles and three RBI in the 1964 Fall Classic.

Bobby Richardson quickly became one of my favorite ballplayers as well. On several occasions, he left tickets for us at Will Call for Saturday afternoon games at the old Comiskey Park on Chicago's south side. After the game we'd drive him back to our Oak Park house, where he'd eat dinner with us and talk baseball, much to the chagrin of our Yankees-hating neighbors. It seemed that every kid on our block was a staunch White Sox fan except for older brother Bill and me, who were Cubs fans.

In those days, it was rare for anyone to root for both the Cubs and White Sox. You loved one and hated the other – it was that simple. I've seen t-shirts that read, "My two favorite teams are the White Sox and whoever is playing the Cubs." And there was no greater White Sox rival during the Fifties and Sixties than the Yankees, so some Cubs fans naturally gravitated toward that incredible dynasty.

Back then, having a major league baseball player come to your

13

house was beyond big. It was huge. It was enormous. It was something I'd anticipate for weeks. When my dad left our house to drive Bobby back to his Chicago hotel on a Saturday night, I'd just sit and stare at the impression Bobby had left in our couch and pretend he was still there. I'd relive every conversation. I just couldn't let it go, such was the even deeper impression the Yankees second baseman had made upon me.

Bobby's first visit to our house was particularly memorable for me. After the Yankees-White Sox game, we waited in the car for a while until a slim, 5-foot-9 man walked up and got in. I guess in the back of my mind I must have assumed that major league baseball players always wore their uniforms wherever they went, so I was clueless as to who this pleasant yet non-descript man in the front seat was. I was also very curious as to why we were now headed away from Comiskey Park before Bobby and his Yankees road uniform featuring jersey No. 1 had strolled triumphantly out of the visiting team's locker room.

Two minutes into the ride home, I blurted out, "Dad, when are we going to pick up Bobby Richardson?" They both had a good laugh at my expense in the front seat, while older brother Bill, in the back seat with me, roared even louder. Then the stranger turned around, stuck his arm over the front seat to shake hands with me and said with a slight Southern drawl, "Hi, Timmy. I'm Bobby Richardson of the New York Yankees. How're you doing today?"

I can't remember my response, if there was one, but I do recall being simultaneously shocked and humiliated. That evening, the neighbor kids snuck up to our living room windows and peered in at Bobby while we talked. They had ridiculed us for having a Yankees player over to our home, but at the same time they were in awe that a real, live major league player was actually sitting in a house on their block.

One of those neighbor kids was Ronnie Miller, who was about

14

four years older than I was. My most vivid memory of this character was a brilliant, over-the-shoulder catch he made one day, a la Willie Mays against Vic Wertz, on a deep fly ball during one of our alley games. What made this play memorable was that he ran into a normally semi-busy street from the alley to make the catch, never looking to see if any cars were coming.

Fortunately none was, and when asked about it later, he said, "I was going to catch that ball no matter what it took, even if it meant getting hit by a car." Wow, I was impressed. The closest I ever came to that type of dedication to the game came about eight years later when I made a grab that cost me 12 stitches in my left arm.

Ernie Banks, who unlike Bobby Richardson never enjoyed the opportunity to play in a World Series, was an easy choice for me when it came to determining my favorite athlete. I followed other sports, but baseball was always number one and Banks was clearly the best player on the Cubs as I was growing up. In addition to hitting home runs and playing a virtually flawless shortstop in the 1950s and early 1960s, Ernie was a breath of fresh air.

Looking back, he was probably the least controversial ballplayer ever. He wore a perpetual smile and always showed the utmost respect for the Cubs ownership, managers and coaches, as well as for umpires, fellow players, the media and fans. Once when goaded into talking about the issue of race in baseball, Ernie responded by saying something along the lines of, "The only race in baseball is the one between the base runner and the baseball."

Perhaps that sounds naïve, and of course Ernie could have used his superstar status to speak out against racial injustice as former players such as Hank Aaron have done. But Banks didn't see himself as a spokesperson for his race, so he didn't pretend to be. All I know is that if everybody shared the enthusiasm, upbeat attitude and respect for others that Ernie displayed, we'd all be a lot better off.

15

Here's a case in point. Try to get your picture taken with a professional athlete sometime, if you haven't already done so. You may get lucky, but more than likely you either won't be able to get physically close enough or you'll get turned down. Of course, the player might sign at a collectibles show in exchange for cash, but other than that, you're probably out of luck.

Growing up in the Fifties and Sixties, it was considerably easier to acquire free autographs from baseball players, but it was still a thrill. One summer, my parents went way beyond the call of duty to make sure we met our heroes up close and personal in order to get those pictures and signatures.

Every year without fail when I was a kid, my parents would drive the entire family nearly 1,000 miles from our suburban Chicago home to Cape May, New Jersey to spend a two-week vacation with our grandparents. It didn't matter how large our family had become or how small our car was – one year seven of us and an acoustic guitar made the grueling trip in a Plymouth Valiant – we always went to stay with Granddad and Mette, who lived in a large, 1865 Victorian house only four blocks from the ocean beaches.

That house is jam-packed with vivid memories. From the screened-in front porch where Granddad would sit on warm summer nights in a wicker rocking chair listening to static-laden Philadelphia Phillies games; to the oven-hot and aptly named Sun Room, where somewhere in the vicinity of 1 billion games of dominoes were played; to a large, bright kitchen where Mette cooked for hours every day and kept her 5,000 jars of vitamins; to a downstairs bathroom roughly the size of a phone booth (except not as tall); to a cozy back bedroom accessible via winding stairs partially hidden behind a refrigerator; to an added second-floor bathroom built on stilts due to the mistrust of plumbing in the mid-1800s; to a couple of third-floor bedrooms where the summer temperatures would reach approximately 500 degrees… this house was incredible.

In the summer of 1970, on our way to Cape May, my parents announced that we were going to make a stop in Philadelphia for a couple of hours. We had been promised that the following year's trip would involve a wonderful detour to Cooperstown, New York and the National Baseball Hall of Fame and Museum. But for right now, younger brother Dave and I were emitting a collective groan as we contemplated being subjected to something as mundane as the Liberty Bell and a bunch of boring historic sites in Philly.

Instead, we eventually pulled into the parking lot of a hotel that some time later was in the news following an outbreak of pneumonia among people attending an American Legion convention. As it turned out, I probably would have been willing to have that serious malady inflicted on me just to experience what our parents had in store for us that day. Little did Dave and I know when we first arrived, but this was the hotel where the Chicago Cubs were staying while in the City of Brotherly Love for a series against the Phillies.

One by one that early afternoon, Cubs players stepped out of the elevator and meandered into the lobby, where my dad quickly corralled them with requests for a photo with his sons and a couple of autographs. Catcher Randy Hundley, outfielder Billy Williams, pitchers Fergie Jenkins and Phil Regan, infielders Ron Santo, Don Kessinger and Glenn Beckert, manager Leo Durocher... it was a dream come true for two love-struck teenagers.

And, of course, the ultimate thrill was meeting Ernie Banks. He looked even taller in person, and his big hands engulfed ours when he greeted us. I have no idea what was going through Ernie's mind when he took a few minutes to talk, have his photo snapped with us and express how great it was to meet us. I'm sure he had done that type of thing thousands of times before. But no matter where his thoughts might have been at that particular moment, he acted as if my brother and I were the two most important people in the world to him, and I'll never forget that as long as I live.

One particular autograph proved more challenging to acquire as Dad diligently worked the room to steer our heroes toward us that day. New Cub Joe Pepitone, in a hurry to meet someone waiting for him outside the hotel, blew off my dad with an excuse about his pinky finger hurting too much to sign.

Dad was not a huge fan of the flamboyant first baseman to begin with, but considered our feelings while telling us Joe didn't want to risk missing that night's game by hurting his finger while writing. We may not have fully believed Dad's explanation, but years later I realized how sensitive he'd been to our feelings, and I really appreciated it. Eventually, Joe re-entered the hotel and this time he signed a couple of autographs and chatted with us.

Our surprise day wasn't over yet. After an early dinner, Dad and Mom topped off one of my most memorable days ever by taking us to old Connie Mack Stadium for the Cubs-Phillies game. My two most vivid recollections from that night are how hideous the advertisements plastered on the outfield walls looked compared to the lush Wrigley Field ivy with which I was familiar, and how Billy Williams' consecutive games played streak of nearly 800 almost came to a screeching halt.

Manager Leo Durocher rested Williams that night, finally inserting him as a pinch-hitter in the ninth inning. But not before we'd seen Sweet Swinging Billy pacing nervously in the dugout. In fact, had either of the batters who preceded him in the ninth inning hit into a double play, we would have witnessed the end of the streak. Billy's streak continued for two more seasons before ending at 1,117 games. As of this writing, it is the sixth longest consecutive games played streak in major league history.

That awesome day was a drop in the ocean compared to everything our parents did for us as we were growing up. I don't have room in this book to even come close to relating everything, but I will mention a couple of things.

My parents became committed Christians shortly before I entered the world, and church was a very significant part of our lives. My dad's philosophy was that Sunday was the Lord's day, and we would go to church for morning and evening services regardless of what else was going on. To borrow a line from Ferris Bueller, a family member would pretty much have to barf up a lung to get out of going.

When I was seven years old, it was too cold for our car to start one Sunday morning and it looked like the arctic weather would be our reprieve from church that day. It wasn't as if I disliked church too much at that point in my life, but my siblings and I certainly would have preferred laying low in the house over getting all bundled up and heading out into the frigid air.

But my dad had a different agenda. Everybody had to put on extra layers of clothing and hop on the sled. Dad, who was 5-foot-7 and 145 pounds, hauled four kids for five blocks on the snow and ice (I'm pretty sure he made my mom walk) and we went to Sunday school and church like always. There couldn't have been more than 15 or 20 people out of a congregation of several hundred in the church sanctuary that day, but the six Boyles were there. Dad was the Billy Williams of church attendees. He just didn't miss a service.

Dad also never allowed an opportunity to slip away to make us happy or turn our disappointments into happiness. And he was especially adept at doing this in connection with baseball. When I was eight, he took Bill and me to a Cubs game at Wrigley Field. We sat on the third base side, about 15 rows behind the Cubs dugout.

At one point in the game, Cubs outfielder Richie Ashburn, who probably hit more foul balls than any other player in the history of the game, stroked a high foul ball in our direction. (By the way, true story. Ashburn once struck the same fan with a foul ball twice in the same at-bat, breaking her nose with the first one and then smacking her as she lay on a stretcher while being carried out of the ballpark… for good measure, I guess.)

19

Everybody in our section stood up as the ball approached. Both my older brother and my dad, who were sitting closer to home plate than I was, reached for it, and I believe it might have deflected off my father's fingertips. It struck the walkway in front of us, rattled off the backs of a couple of seats and bounced under the railing, finally coming to rest by my feet.

I looked down in shock, realizing that a coveted souvenir was within my grasp. I flung my hand toward the ball, but just as I was about to grab it, another kid from a nearby seat reached in and snatched it away. I was crushed. I broke into tears and my dad spent an entire inning consoling me. (Rudely, Ashburn failed to immediately launch another foul ball in our direction.)

Lamenting my misfortunate, I laid down on the living room floor of our Oak Park home that evening. How could God have allowed somebody else to snag the baseball that was clearly designed to be mine?

Unbeknownst to me, while I pawed at the carpet with my fingers, envisioning a baseball in my grip and chastising myself for not grabbing it before someone else could, Dad was using his digits to type a letter to Ashburn, explaining what happened and how disappointed his son was. About two weeks later, a box came in the mail for me. It contained a baseball autographed by Richie Ashburn, accompanied by a personal note.

Third Inning

Sweet as Honey

Here's how whacked I was as a seven-year-old kid. This is how obsessed I was with baseball and the Cubs. Every school day, the afternoon bus would drop me off on the corner of Madison Street and Home Avenue in Oak Park, Illinois, exactly four, tree-lined blocks from our two-story house.

Ours was the last house, with only a narrow street, a fence and a grassy knoll separating us from the busy Eisenhower Expressway. Actually, for the first five or six years of my life, the deep gulley that eventually became the Ike was a huge, open expanse of dirt, grass, weeds, rocks and broken bottles leading to several sets of train tracks.

Of course, my parents wouldn't allow us to go near it, and since Mom could clearly see that gulley from a side window of the house, we rarely risked it. But I couldn't resist taking a stroll in that direction the week before they opened the expressway. The wide road was completed, but wasn't officially open for business yet.

A bunch of us would-be thugs wandered down there one day – past a variety of signs telling people not to wander down there – and laid on our backs on the smooth, dry road. So clean, and without any cracks, it looked almost futuristic.

"This is the last time we'll ever be able to do this, so enjoy it while you can," one of the older kids proclaimed. "If you try this in a few days, you'll get splattered by a Mack truck and they'll have to scoop up your guts with a shovel."

I shuddered for a moment after hearing that statement. But soon it became very quiet and peaceful, just lying there on the newly-

21

hardened cement and staring up at big white clouds slowly drifting across the bright blue sky. Sure enough, within a week the cars and trucks started whizzing by, making so much noise that the inside of our house sometimes sounded like a factory. I think that's when my parents decided it was time to get out of Dodge.

But before we moved, that four-block walk every school day in the spring and early fall was memorable for me because I created a game that I played faithfully on my way home after getting off the bus. I would pretend the Cubs were squaring off at Wrigley Field against some team – I'd generally choose whichever team they were playing that day in real life – and the game was heading into the top of the eighth inning with the score tied.

However many cars passed me going in either direction while I walked that first block, that's how many runs the opponent would score in the top of the eighth inning. The number of cars that drove past me during the second block represented how many runs the Cubs tallied in the bottom of the eighth, and so forth.

Being a Cubs fanatic, I'd walk as swiftly as possible during the first and third blocks when Chicago's opponent was up to bat, and as slowly as necessary during the second and fourth blocks in order to give the Cubs more time to score and the best chance to win. Any neighbor watching this daily, one-kid parade must have assumed I tired very easily.

As a little squirt, there was a limit to how fast I could move, especially while carrying books and a lunch box. So, sometimes an unexpected and unwelcomed rush of traffic on the first or third block would enable the Cubs' foe to take a commanding lead. But I knew how to take care of that problem. I'd practically crawl that last block if necessary to allow enough cars to pass by and ensure a Cubs victory. One time I had to sit outside my house for 30 minutes in the cold rain (there were no rainouts in this game) before a car cruised by to give the Cubs their winning run.

My mom yelled out that I'd catch pneumonia if I didn't come inside the house that instant, but I screamed that the Cubs needed another run and how could she not understand how much more important that was than the risk of getting sick. She just shook her head and sighed.

I don't remember my final four-block walk on Home Avenue during the spring of 1961 – nor whether the Cubs won or lost that last imaginary game – but I do recall how much I missed playing it. That summer, my parents dropped a bombshell on us by announcing that the family was moving from Oak Park to Wheaton in a couple of months. It was a 20-mile move, straight west, but it might as well have been to another country as far as I was concerned.

In addition to losing all my friends, everything about my world that was familiar would be gone… the front steps of our house where we fired a rubber ball and fielded the ricochet a thousand times a day, the dirty yet beloved alley where we gladly donated blood, sweat and tears while playing every sport imaginable, my tiny bedroom where I received the occasional solitude I needed and where I dreamed about becoming a major league baseball player, our garage with the basketball hoop and rusted backboard, the memory-filled classrooms and gymnasium at the Lutheran school I had attended since kindergarten…

The move was one of the most traumatic events of my life. Nowadays we have psychologists to tell us how unsettling a family relocation can be for an eight-year-old. Back then, nobody thought much about it. Except for the eight-year-old kid.

The worst thing about moving, for me anyway, was the unknown. To this day, leaving a comfort zone to enter any foreign realm makes me uneasy. I thrive on routine. I know it sounds monotonous, but I'd be perfectly content doing pretty much the same thing in the same way almost every day. It started very early in life. Anything out of the ordinary – whether at home or school – made me extremely uncomfortable.

23

When my mom would attend parent-teacher conferences, they'd tell her I was an above average student who was well behaved and didn't cause any trouble but who, nearly every morning, insisted on knowing the day's schedule. And if my teachers deviated from that plan, I'd pipe in with something like, "But don't you remember you said we'd review our math homework at 10 a.m.? It's only 9:56." They probably wanted to strangle me – which back then a teacher could get away with now and then, especially at a private school – but I just didn't want any surprises.

Maybe it's one of the reasons I love baseball so much. It's a very predictable sport. You can only guess who's going to pitch or hit well on any given night, and you don't know which team is going to win. But day in and day out during the season, players take the field and play virtually the same game they've been playing for more than 140 years in an almost identical manner.

Some people would say that's boring. In fact, I've heard baseball called the most boring sport in the world. No, make that the most boring *activity* in the world. Sometimes a family member will walk into the TV room while I'm watching a game and say in an exaggerated voice, "Wow, it's already 2-1 and they're only in the eighth inning! How exciting!" Needless to say, they don't appreciate a pitcher's duel. I used to try to explain that sometimes baseball games are high scoring and sometimes they're low scoring and a lot of times they're somewhere in between. But it just never got through.

Every once in a while, they'll actually sit down and watch five minutes of a game with me. But unless someone hits a home run or there's a bench-clearing brawl, they'll get up, shake their head and mumble something about how "nothing ever happens in this stupid sport." Nothing ever happens?!?!

I don't bother explaining that on every single pitch there are hundreds of "things happening." Catchers are giving pitch and location signals, pitchers are nodding their agreement or shaking off the sign,

24

outfielders are shading to their left or right, infielders are "cheating" toward the bag or away from it, on-deck hitters are studying the pitcher's delivery, batters are guessing fastball, curve, slider or changeup, managers are contemplating moves they won't make for several innings, and base coaches are comparing opposing outfielders' arm strengths to their base runners' speed.

On a lighter note, there's lots of other stuff going on as well. Bullpen catchers are determining how much longer they can doze before a call might come for them to warm up a pitcher, and some fans are deciding whether to buy another beer. Which reminds me of an episode from *The Simpsons*.

After embarrassing himself at a party, Homer agrees to quit drinking for a month and Marge is holding him to it. Unfortunately, Homer's month coincides with a company outing at the ballpark. Looking around and seeing hundreds of fans smiling broadly while consuming Duff beer, a sober and somber Homer shakes his head and sadly declares – in agreement with my family members – "I never realized how boring this game is." (By the way, if any of you *Simpsons* fans are tempted to let me know that I left out a detail or a word in that scenario, number one, thanks for the input; and number two, get a life.)

Many marginal baseball fans will say that beer is the one thing that can make the sport interesting, or at least tolerable. But that could be said for pretty much anything you find boring, including most parties. All I can say is that if you need beer to appreciate baseball, you don't really know the game.

I have a friend named Jerry who is not a big sports fan, but who does take pleasure in watching baseball. I asked him once why he likes a sport that he never played much and which can sometimes go on for hours without eliciting a great deal of excitement.

"It's very simple," Jerry told me. "There's no time clock. In the other major sports, the clock is a constant reminder that time is slipping away, and that nagging feeling is so unnerving that it keeps me from enjoying the game. But with baseball, there's always time to catch up. All you have to do is score enough runs before making your final out. It might take a few minutes or a few hours, but there's always time to get the job done." Of course, I have to take Jerry's thoughts with a grain of salt because he also likes to drink a lot of beer.

It took me a long time to make friends after we moved to Wheaton. Everybody seemed so different. It was much more suburban than urban, and that required some getting used to. Our house was small – if you had more than four people in the living room you'd start feeling claustrophobic – but adequate, and our front and back yards were bigger than in Oak Park, but not huge.

We didn't have an alley behind our house, but there wasn't a great deal of traffic on our street so we were able to play baseball, touch football and hockey in it. Neighbors who'd grown accustomed to parking their cars in the street changed their habits quickly after we moved in and began an airborne onslaught of baseballs, footballs and hockey pucks.

One thing I adapted to quite well was playing baseball on grass rather than in an alley. We were more than willing to walk or ride our bikes four blocks to a large field next to the elementary school brother Dave and I were now attending in order to play ball there. The grass felt so soft under my feet after running non-stop in the Oak Park alley for several years. It's not like we'd never seen grass in Oak Park – after all, sometimes a few blades would peek through cracks in the alley cement – but we'd certainly never played on a field this large before.

Two major league players from whom I derived great satisfaction while watching them smack baseballs out of the park – Eddie Mathews of the Milwaukee Braves and Ernie Banks of the Chicago Cubs – both hit exactly 512 home runs in their careers. Big deal. I hit that many homers almost every summer from the age of 12 to about 16 or so. Of course, we were playing whiffle ball, but so what?

One of the advantages of playing on teams consisting of only three to four players is that you are pretty much guaranteed to bat at least once an inning and often several times. Because we averaged four whiffle ball games per day (two before lunch and a pair after) at least five days a week, weather permitting, the stats piled up.

Plus, we cheated. After dinner in the summer, we had to stick around close to the house. Because there was no field in the immediate vicinity, we'd play home run derby in the street. One guy with a wooden bat (we didn't have aluminum bats back then) would toss a tennis ball or rubber ball in the air and belt it as far as he could. If it passed a designated line down the street on the fly without being caught, it was considered a homer.

The more fielders there were, the more difficult it was to hit a home run. Adding a significant challenge to the feat was the rule that the ball had to land in the street, not on the grassy parkways, sidewalks, front yards, house roofs or neighbors' heads. So, when there were a lot of fielders, you either had to belt it a great distance past all of them or hit a line drive that would drop untouched just over the home run line. In order to make sure we accumulated staggering home run figures by the end of the summer, we'd count each of these homers among our whiffle ball totals.

Our move from Oak Park to Wheaton coincided almost precisely with my transfer from older brother Bill to younger brother Dave, as far as hanging out was concerned. Bill was a freshman in high school when we made the move, and I quickly learned that it wasn't cool for freshmen to keep company with third graders. He would still play some indoor games with me when the weather was bad or help me with homework now and then, but he spent most of his time outside of the house with friends.

Dave was only four years old when we moved to Wheaton, but within a year or so he was showing some serious aptitude when it came to sports. I was four years older than Dave, so I took it upon myself to help him learn how to play a variety of sports. And I told myself I would never treat him the way I'd been treated by older kids in Oak Park. But before long I would break that vow.

Dave, who we nicknamed "The Peach" one summer because his new crew-cut resembled peach fuzz, was the sweetest kid you'd ever want to meet. A little short for his age and somewhat stocky compared to his skinny older brothers, he had deep, penetrating eyes and dark brown hair. Dave was pretty quiet for the most part, and he actually listened to what others and I told him.

This quality made him a good learner, and by the age of five he had already developed a very fluid swing from the left side. In fact, when you delivered a pitch in his zone – low and directly over the plate – he'd often golf it to the fence at the other side of our yard. Once he reached age seven, we started working on his fielding, and again he adapted quickly. Even though he was left-handed, he learned how to play all the infield positions competently, and soon acquired the knack of deftly hauling in fly balls as an outfielder as well.

Here was a typical summer day for brother Dave and me after we reached the ages of eight and 12, respectively. We'd get up whenever we woke up, which was usually around 8:30 a.m. or so. After struggling with the weighty decision regarding which t-shirt to wear with our blue jeans – we didn't wear shorts, even on the hottest days, because we assumed we were going to have to slide several times per game and shorts might put a damper on doing what it took to win – we'd have a leisurely breakfast of Rice Krispies or Cheerios with honey and milk, a piece of toast with honey and ground-up sunflower seeds, and maybe a banana or raisins.

I don't think I saw a bowl of white sugar until I was about 12 years old. It was taboo in our house, and to this day I almost never use sugar for anything. Honey was big in our family, mainly due to my grandmother, Mette. A health food fanatic, she was tall and thin and could out-work most men. My grandfather was in poor physical shape when he married her in 1944, and slowly but surely she nursed him back to health.

This occasionally required slapping "inappropriate" food, i.e. anything with sugar in it, out of his hands before it could reach his mouth. If it wasn't natural, Granddad had to have a very good excuse for eating it, such as being forced at gunpoint. I'm sure he often resented Mette's Gestapo methods, but he ended up living to 101 without any major health problems along the way, so who could argue with her methods? Mette reached the ripe old age of 103, by the way, and during her last five years or so was always ready with an "I told you so" for anyone who cared to listen.

Granddad, who stood a tall-for-his-time 6-foot-1 and had a face that was about as intimidating as Winnie-the-Pooh's, would sometimes playfully make fun of Mette when she wasn't within ear shot, just to entertain us. And occasionally he'd do something directly in front of her that would nearly floor us with laughter.

One summer evening during the Sixties we were on the boardwalk in Cape May, New Jersey when he bought a cup of orange juice while she was off using the restroom. (At least that's what Mette *said* she was doing. For all I know, she might have been stealing sugar packets from outdoor café tables and throwing them into the ocean so that people wouldn't be poisoned by them.) Well, she came back just as he was starting to drink it and quickly stomped up to the guy who had sold it to him, demanding to know if it was freshly squeezed juice.

When the quivering man admitted it was not, she turned to Granddad and shrieked, "It's not freshly squeezed! It's not freshly squeezed!" Instead of swallowing his mouthful and dutifully handing Mette the cup to dispose of as she saw fit, he dramatically spit the orange juice over the boardwalk railing and onto the sand, then threw the cup in a trash can in mock anger while glaring at the vendor as if he'd been betrayed.

We also weren't allowed to eat sugary items when on our own away from the house, and while this was more difficult for my parents to monitor, they did a good job of instilling enough guilt in us to make it a difficult choice on many occasions. The most challenging aspect for me in this area was resisting the nearly overwhelming urge to jam that rock-hard slab of pink bubble gum in my mouth whenever I opened a pack of Topps baseball cards.

Several of us would walk a couple of blocks to the corner drug store in Wheaton at least once a day during baseball season to purchase some five-cent Topps packs. Topps was the only sports trading card company for most of the 1960s, and that lack of competition enabled the company to get away with producing some rather bland sets of cards through the years until Upper Deck came along and revolutionized the hobby in the late 1980s with high-end cards. Topps then rallied to put out some impressive high-end sets of its own.

But back then we didn't care about the cardboard quality because we didn't know any better. We loved Topps cards and there wasn't much else on which I would rather have spent my allowance. We knew there was always a chance we could find an Ernie Banks or Willie Mays or Al Kaline or Mickey Mantle card whenever we opened a pack. And even if we didn't chew the gum, its pungent odor that we loved would stay embedded in the cards for weeks.

Anytime the neighbor kids caught wind of the fact that Dave and I were heading to the store to buy baseball cards, they'd drop whatever they were doing and rush to join us. They knew there was a very good chance that either Dave or I – and if they were really lucky, both of us – would hand over his gum to them.

The only thing better than trying to chew one of those pieces of pink plywood was cramming two or three of them into your mouth at one time. After about six hours of grinding multiple slabs of gum with your teeth, you could eventually form it into a ball and tuck it into your cheek with your tongue. Then you could pretend you were Bill

Mazeroski of the Pittsburgh Pirates or Nellie Fox of the Chicago White Sox, a pair of second basemen known for always having huge wads of tobacco in their cheeks.

We were told that Topps produced the same number of cards for every player, but somehow I ended up with about 80 Felix Mantilla cards for every one I'd find depicting Mickey Mantle. Like many kids, I'd organize my cards by team and tightly wrap a thick rubber band around each group, ideally with a team card at the top. Then I'd shove them into a cardboard box, never dreaming that if I took better care of them they'd someday be worth a lot more than the penny per card I paid for them.

I never really got into card flipping like a lot of kids, but we'd often create games that required considerable handling of our cards, serving to soften and eventually round off the corners. Sometimes I'd even grab one of my dad's fountain pens and write on a card.

One year I decided to apply glue to the backs of some of my cards and form a scrapbook. Fortunately, I grew tired of this tedious activity after pasting the Baltimore Orioles and Boston Red Sox cards against colored paper. (Even back then I was obsessed about doing things in alphabetical order.) To this day, I have a Ted Williams card from the late 1950s, and all you can see on the back of his card is the red construction paper to which I glued it. In mint condition, that card is valued at several hundred dollars. Mine is not worth jack... except to me.

I'm one of the lucky people whose parents did not throw away his baseball cards after he moved out of the house. In the late 1970s, after learning that cards from the 1950s and 1960s had become valuable, I drove to my parents' house and rejoiced after finding all of our old baseball cards still tucked away in shoeboxes on a shelf near the sump pump.

I was elated until I learned that while discovering them was

31

better than not finding them, the poor condition of many of those old cards seriously decreased their value. Over time, however, I was happy I had not preserved our cards in pristine condition. If I had, I'm sure I would have sold them and blown the money. Now their sentimental value is worth much more to me than whatever funds I might have gained by selling them.

Back to our typical summer day routine. After breakfast, Dave and I would hang outside our house, waiting for whoever wanted to play whiffle ball that day to show up. Once we had six to eight guys, we'd head over to the field on our bikes, well stocked with full water bottles, whiffle balls and bats, and a slew of torn-up white sheets.

Upon arriving at the field, it was always my job to "line" the outfield from one foul line to the other with these strips of sheets that would designate our outfield "wall." I'd configure these outfield walls depending on my mood and the wind direction that day, and this authority made me absolutely drunk with power. If the wind was blowing in, I wouldn't make the wall as deep, but if it was blowing out, I'd move the strips farther back. And if it was calm that morning, I'd make the wall shallow or deep based on whether I was up for high- or low-scoring games.

With the exception of brother Dave, we were all natural right-handed hitters. But in order to keep the scores more like baseball than football, we older kids agreed to bat left-handed in the first through third and seventh through ninth innings. It was slow-pitch whiffle ball, and with no called strikes, you could pretty much wait for your perfect pitch before teeing off.

Throughout the course of a game, we'd frequently engage in the highly intelligent banter of pre-teens. "What was wrong with that pitch, jerk face?" a pitcher would inquire incredulously of a batter who had let a pitch go by without swinging, perhaps tossing in a few colorful adjectives. "Well, for one, you threw it, nimrod," the batter would retort. "You wouldn't know a good pitch if it bit you in the butt," an

32

infielder would chime in. And on it would go until every player on one team had insulted every player on the other.

Because there were only three or four guys on a team most of the time, anything hit on the ground was pitcher's hands out. So on sharp grounders past an infielder, the outfielder would race in at breakneck speed while the pitcher ran toward him. After scooping up the grounder, the outfielder would fire it to the rapidly approaching pitcher, who would yell "out" the split second he caught the throw. In the meantime, the batter would yell "safe" as he touched first base. There were numerous heated arguments in every game, and when somebody in the field got really ticked off, the next batter could count on several fastballs honing in on his head.

You might not think a whiffle ball could hurt much, even when thrown at high velocity, but you really had to get hit by one to realize it did. We never liked the typical whiffle balls with holes in them. Fine for throwing dipping and diving curves, especially on windy days, they were difficult to get a bead on as a fielder because the wind so easily cut through them, knocking down rockets one day and sending popups spiraling toward the outfield wall the next.

Instead, we preferred the plastic balls without holes. When one of them suffered a crack, we'd repair it with black masking tape. If you connected with one of those taped babies, it could go a long way. On the other hand, if it struck your arm, back or face when thrown at top speed by an angry pitcher, it could cause a nasty welt. That type of occurrence was often followed by a batter whipping his plastic bat at the pitcher and then charging the mound if he thought he could slip in a few punches before the fight was broken up.

Wouldn't you think that a kid who had been terrified of being yelled at while playing sports in an Oak Park alley every day would go out of his way to be kind to younger kids after moving to a grass field in Wheaton? Alas, I'm afraid I wasn't always the role model I should have been. From the age of 12 to about 15 or so, I'd never hesitate to yell at a

33

younger kid for making an error or not hustling on a play. I wasn't nearly as brutal toward them as what I'd experienced at their age, but the whole situation would have been much more pleasant for them, including brother Dave, if I had learned my lesson and been an encourager instead of a criticizer.

Dave was a slightly better ballplayer than I had been at his age. My dad had trained him to bat and throw left-handed from day one, and he acquired a very natural stroke as he learned how to hit. He was also an exceptional fielder. But one summer, Dave got really lazy… or so it seemed.

I'd be on the mound trying to break off some curveballs to the hitter and I'd look out in right field and see Dave lying down. He'd rise to a sitting position as the ball was being delivered in case he had to stand up and make a play, but then would lie down again if the ball wasn't hit toward him. At bat, he'd swing for the fences every time, and if he hit the ball on the ground, he'd lope casually to first base. He'd also complain of a sore throat every day.

The situation kept getting worse, and suddenly Dave went from the guy you'd want on your team to the guy you'd want on the other squad. All the older kids – including me – were, of course, very sympathetic. We yelled at him daily for dogging it, but he was usually too tired to respond.

Occasionally between innings, a couple of the older guys would try to hit him with thrown or batted balls as he lay in the outfield, which I'm sure he appreciated. Just to show Dave how seriously angry we were at him for his ongoing listlessness, we'd make him lug most of the equipment back home after the games on his bike, loading up those attractive side baskets with water bottles and placing bets regarding whether he'd make it up the steep hill adjacent to the field without falling off.

Finally, one late July morning, my mom announced that Dave

wasn't playing whiffle ball that day because she was taking him to thedoctor. As it turned out, a blood test revealed he had mononucleosis. That meant six weeks of rest at home, and certainly explained why he hadn't exactly been Charlie Hustle the past month or so. When I announced Dave's condition to the other guys at the field the next day, we all felt guilty for screaming at him... for about 30 seconds. Then we rushed to get in as many games as we could, sans Dave, before school started up again in early September.

Dave knew his whiffle ball season was over for the year, and we figured ours was finished as well once the school bells began ringing again. But we lucked out and were blessed with a beautiful fall Saturday afternoon about a month later when nobody was forced to do chores at home. So, we decided to wrap up the season with a whiffle ball double-header.

After considerable begging, Dave convinced Mom and Dad to allow him to come watch us, but not play. I was under strict orders to bring him home immediately if he showed any sign of fatigue. I had no idea what "fatigue" was, nor did I care. All I knew was I had thought the whiffle balls and bats would stay in hibernation until spring, and here we were getting one more chance to play.

Dave, who received a standing ovation from the six or seven of us before the first of the two games, served as the umpire for Game 1. Bored out of his mind with that job, he lobbied me to let him play in the "nightcap" and I reluctantly agreed. Making matters worse, he ended up being my teammate in that second game.

Dave hadn't swung a bat or thrown a ball in six weeks, and while his rust showed in the first few innings, he began whacking the ball in the middle frames. We trailed by three runs heading into the bottom of the ninth in what would be our last inning of whiffle ball for the year, barring extra innings. We loaded the bases with one out and started envisioning ending the season with a come-from-behind win. With the chance to be a hero, I swung mightily but popped out. It was now up to Dave, and this time he didn't need to worry about anyone yelling at him if he didn't come through.

"Just a single to keep it going, Dave. That's all we need," I shouted.

Dave took a couple of pitches before finding one to his liking. He then ripped a pitch so far beyond our makeshift right field wall that the outfielder didn't even budge. Dave's grand slam gave us a one-run victory and we mobbed him at home plate after he completed his leisurely trot around the bases, milking it for all it was worth. The guys on the losing team also joined in the celebration once they finished throwing their gloves on the ground and insulting their pitcher for giving up a game-winning dinger to an invalid.

Even back then I was well aware that it was only a whiffle ball game, and I'm sure nobody else who participated that day remembers it… except maybe Dave. But as I thought back on my temporary disappointment for failing to come through right before Dave's heroics, I realized fate had stepped in that day and I was so glad I made an out.

"The Peach" really needed a boost, and to cap off a whiffle ball season like that after all the grief and sickness and blood tests he'd gone through during the summer, well, that sure was a sweet way to end it.

Fourth Inning

Be Ready

The last thing I expected on that fateful Sunday morning was the pastor calling out my name and asking me to come up to the platform. I was sitting in one of the first few pews on the left side of the sanctuary with the other first graders, as we always did during the first 30 minutes of the morning church service before being dismissed to our Sunday school classes in the basement.

I can't remember if I had been paying attention to what the reverend was talking about – probably not – or whether I was chatting with my "neighbor" or, more likely, trying to remember whether Don Cardwell and Dick Ellsworth were slated as the Cubs' starting pitchers in that afternoon's double-header. But once my name was called, all activity and whispers in our section halted immediately.

"Mr. Boyle will now come up to tell us about this exciting new program," the pastor bellowed.

The Sunday school teachers at our non-denominational church in Oak Park, Illinois always referred to us as Mr. or Miss, followed by our last names. I guess they wanted us to act like little adults rather than seven-year-old kids, but that's how I knew the pastor was referring to me.

What exciting new program? I wondered, my face turning beet red as I hesitantly rose from my seat and started squeezing past my fellow first graders with their little legs sticking up past the end of the pew and their little feet blocking my every step. *What could Pastor Breeden possibly want me to say up there?*

I was as fearful as I was astonished, but I knew there was no choice. Despite suddenly feeling nauseous and with blood rushing to my head, I had to go up to the platform in front of hundreds of people. It seemed like everyone was staring at me, and as I dared to make eye contact with a few of the adult parishioners once I finally entered the aisle, I noticed an increasing number of smiles, followed by outright laughter that grew in volume the closer I got to the platform. It felt like a nightmare that had turned into reality.

Great, I thought. *It's not bad enough that I have to walk up to the platform and stand in front of a bunch of people not knowing what I'm going to say. No, they have to make it worse by laughing at me and humiliating me before I even get up there.*

As I started to mount the five carpeted steps toward the pulpit, I was surprised to see my dad within a few feet of me, walking in the exact same direction. He too had a huge grin on his face as he reached out to my trembling body and held me close to him. Once at the top of the platform, Dad waited for what seemed like an eternity for all the laughter echoing across the auditorium to finally subside while I just stood there staring blankly, wondering what I'd done to deserve this.

"Looks like I've got some help with this announcement," my dad said to an appreciative audience.

Suddenly it dawned on me. "Mr. Boyle" was my father, not me. I wasn't supposed to be up here. I could have stayed seated in the pew and everything would have been fine. I snuck a glance at my classmates, who were just now grasping the irony of the situation and were laughing like stupid little hyenas. *I'm going to hear about this for a long time*, I thought.

Fifty-six years later, I'd gladly suffer an embarrassment of that magnitude if the end result were having my dad put his arm around me again. He passed away on March 8, 1999, the same day that Joe DiMaggio died. Dad had contracted progressive supranuclear palsy about five years previously at age 76, and the deterioration was slow

38

but steady. It didn't help that he was originally misdiagnosed with Parkinson's disease.

My siblings and I first noticed the effects of his illness while driving in a car behind him on the way to Cape May, New Jersey from a dinner we'd attended at a country club in Medford, where my aunt and uncle were members. Dad was very subtly drifting from his lane into others and then pulling back to where he belonged during the entire 90-minute drive. We knew it wasn't the influence of alcohol because he never drank. We figured he was either tired or was just starting to get too old to drive as well as he used to. My mom must have been half-asleep in the passenger seat next to him because when we told her about it later, she said she hadn't noticed.

Stiffness, awkward movements and a lack of balance started manifesting themselves a few months later, and within a couple of years Dad was having trouble walking. Actually, for quite a while he was only having trouble *starting* to walk. His first few steps were almost always very shaky, stutter steps, and often his upper body would get ahead of his feet and down he'd go. Seemed like every week Mom was calling us from the Florida home where they'd retired to tell us that Dad had fallen headfirst into a table or chair or wall. When we'd fly there for a visit, he'd invariably have about 10 bandages on various parts of his face, arms and legs.

But once he got going, Dad could really cruise. We'd be walking with him in the courtyard of their retirement village, and after making sure he didn't bite the dust on those first four or five steps, it was sometimes difficult to keep up with him, even though he was approaching his 79th birthday. Dad knew that if he slowed down, he'd have to go through that whole awkward and embarrassing process again, and that was the last thing he wanted to do. So, he wouldn't stop until he had to.

Eventually he couldn't walk at all. That disease just eats away at you. After struggling with a walker for a while, he took a seat in a wheelchair and never walked again. During his last couple of years, Mom took care of Dad like he was an infant. Changing his adult diapers, replacing sheets, preparing drinks in non-spill cups, responding quickly every time he'd beckon her by tapping a yardstick on the bed frame… she was an absolute saint and never complained about it.

Come to think of it, Dad never complained either, despite the fact that his disease made him more uncomfortable and more dependent on Mom every day. He merely accepted his fate, continued to thank God for all the healthy years he had enjoyed and carried on the best he could.

One time near the end when he was lying in bed, I lay down next to him and gently stroked his thick shock of white hair, just like he'd done to me when I was sick as a child. He wasn't talking much at that point, but perhaps sensing my concern, he said in a cracking voice, "You know, son, there really isn't much pain. It really doesn't hurt. It's just sort of numb most of the time."

Midway through his 81st year, the family started discussing the inevitable, hoping we wouldn't have to make a decision regarding how long he'd live. Dad had made it clear while still communicative that he didn't want to be kept alive through artificial means. Once he couldn't swallow anymore, the decision to cut off the temporary feeding tube was a no-brainer, albeit difficult. The doctor told us that my dad would probably live one week after the tubes were disconnected. We had them removed at 6 p.m. on a Monday and he died at 6:10 p.m. the following Monday. The doctor's prediction was off by 10 minutes.

Those seven days might as well have been 100. Walking back and forth from Mom and Dad's condo – now just Mom's, I guess – over and over again to sit with him while he lay there in what I hope was a mostly incoherent state was an exercise in frustration, sadness, anger, depression and exhaustion.

A big part of me wondered why we spare our animals this kind of discomfort and pain, but not our humans. One shot and it's over for a cat or dog that can't function on its own anymore. For a human who wants nothing more than to die, it's one week of dehydration, starvation, cramps and fear.

There were two things that kept us all sane that week as Dad lay there dying. One was closeness of family. We were truly bonded together like never before. My two brothers, my sister and I were all there for the same reason – to support our mom and say our goodbyes to a father who had spent pretty much every waking moment of his adult life working to support us and trying to teach us to focus on the most important things in life.

My dad had a favorite phrase he used to bark out at me when I was up to bat, regardless of whether it was a Little League game, a high school game or a church league softball game. "Be ready," he'd always say. Be ready. If you had known my dad, you'd realize that the phrase had all sorts of connotations to it.

For that immediate situation, it meant be ready for the next pitch. Focus. Concentrate. Nothing mattered more than that next pitch. Be ready for a fastball. Be ready for a curve. Don't guess, just be ready for whatever comes your way. Off the field, "be ready" was an unspoken mantra with Dad. He looked at life as being extremely significant, but also very temporary. He believed that being ready for the next life was the single most important thing you could do in this life. Over the years, I came to agree with him.

The other thing that kept us from going completely nuts that week was the comfort we gained from knowing Dad was all set to meet his Maker. Actually, he'd been ready for a long time. He had made his peace with God many years before and was living for the sole purpose of pleasing Him. The only thing better than living for God, in Dad's mind, was living *with* Him. I guess Dad had earned the right to tell me to "be ready." He was ready well before he got sick.

41

* * *

Prior to my birth, Dad was a business manager for the minor league baseball Terre Haute, Indiana Phillies in the old 3-I League (Iowa, Illinois and Indiana). He had been a baseball fanatic while growing up in Collingswood, New Jersey and had taken a job as a bank clerk following high school. After serving in World War II and reaching the level of Major, he returned to the States and again worked in a bank. But deposits, withdrawals, loans and interest were not in his blood. Baseball was.

He wrote a letter to the general manager of every major league baseball team – there were 16 at the time – saying that while he did not have any experience in professional baseball, he possessed an unbounded passion for the game and would do just about anything to land a job in the sport. Rejection letter after rejection letter came his way in the ensuing weeks. If only those GMs had seen first-hand my dad's limitless enthusiasm for the sport back in the summer of 1934.

As a senior in high school, he and a friend hitchhiked from South Jersey to New York City to attend the second-ever All-Star Game, held at the Polo Grounds. He kept the scorecard from the game, which is now one of my prized possessions. That was the game in which National League pitcher Carl Hubbell struck out five consecutive batters, including Babe Ruth, Lou Gehrig and Jimmie Foxx.

Well, at least one of those baseball executives seemed to understand. Dad received a phone call from a high-ranking official with the Philadelphia Phillies, asking if he could come in for an interview. Soon, my parents and sister Carol were on their way to Terre Haute to fulfill Dad's dreams of a career in professional baseball.

My dad thought he'd hit the big time, but in reality it was merely another step leading him to his ultimate goal – one he didn't yet realize he had. After being with the Phillies minor league team for a few years, Dad started to feel some disillusionment. World War II had

42

delayed meeting his daughter until she was 2, and now a considerable amount of time at the ballpark and travel with the team was taking its toll on Mom, Carol and three-year-old Billy at home.

In February 1951, Dad went with the Phillies to spring training in Florida for a month while Mom took the kids to their grandmother's home in Philadelphia. While away from his wife and family, Dad had plenty of time to think. He couldn't seem to get that nagging, "Is this all there is?" feeling out of his mind. *How could I feel so unfulfilled when I'm finally working at a job in professional baseball, something I've always wanted for my life?* he wondered.

He was also becoming increasingly uncomfortable with the tight bond between alcohol and professional baseball, as well as with the way his immediate superiors took advantage of his sobriety by pressuring him to accompany them and serve as a designated driver during their bar-hopping evenings.

Back home in Terre Haute in late March, a few days ahead of the family, Dad was flipping the dial on his radio when he came across a station featuring a local pastor. It seemed to my dad that the reverend was speaking directly to him, addressing his very issues. When Mom and the kids returned from Philly, Dad announced, "We're going to a new church this Sunday."

Over time, my parents crossed the line of faith and Christianity became a relationship and a lifestyle rather than merely a religion. Instead of easing his mind, however, the immediate results of that spiritual decision seemed to instill in Dad an even deeper sense that there might be something else out there waiting for him.

"Maybe baseball just isn't where I'm supposed to be," he told Mom. Soon he heard about a job opening at a new monthly magazine published by Moody Bible Institute in Chicago. To the surprise of all his baseball buddies, he announced that he was leaving the sport that had been number one in his life to follow the orders of a new manager.

43

"You'll never be able to get back into baseball, you know," he was told. "When this religious phase of yours passes and you want to come back, you won't be able to."

Dad just smiled and made plans to move to Chicago. And he never looked back. Thirty-plus years later, the family attended a retirement luncheon in honor of my father's service at Moody. We all knew that Dad was considered a nice guy and was well liked, but until we heard personal story after story from the people he worked with regarding the many things he had done for them – notes of encouragement, visits during illnesses, comforting calls, prayers in times of need and many more – we didn't fully understand how selfless he was.

After everybody finished praising him, it was Dad's turn to say a few words at the podium. (This time I stayed in my seat when his name was announced.) As usual, he set up his talk with a quaint story.

"A little boy refused to eat his broccoli at dinner one night," Dad began, "despite repeated threats from his parents that he'd have to go to bed immediately and would not get his dessert if he continued his insubordination. That was fine with the boy, whose appetite had been quashed by the sight and smell of the distasteful vegetable. So off he marched to bed.

"Later that night, a tremendous storm struck, with crashing thunder and dramatic lightning. The boy crawled out of bed, opened the window and yelled, 'Hey, God, all this fuss over a few vegetables?'

"Well," Dad continued after some hearty laughter, "that's how I feel right now. Why all this fuss over a few years of service?"

It was vintage Dad. Modesty with a playful air to it. He was the type who would tell "jokes" that must have been culled from a Norman Rockwell calendar, such was their innocence and wholesomeness. Such as, "Today's weather report – Six inches of snow, followed by little boys on sleds." Depending on the response of his audience, he would also quip, "My jokes are nothing to laugh about."

Imagine living in your home for the first 18 years of your life and never once hearing your dad utter one profanity, see him consume one alcoholic drink or smoke one cigarette or cigar, or hear him tell one off-color joke. I didn't realize how remarkable that was until I started hanging out at friends' houses when I reached junior high school age.

That's when I began to comprehend that my dad was something special. Of course, there were times when he overdid it. You'd be standing with him outside and four planes would fly overhead in formation and he'd say something like, "Matthew, Mark, Luke and John." Or somebody famous would die and while the rest of the family was eulogizing him or her, Dad would wonder aloud where that person would be spending eternity.

As a high school and college student, stuff like that really bugged me. I thought my dad's "religion" had pushed him off the deep end. Even though I believed the same basics regarding Christianity that he did, I had no desire to reach that level of "spirituality." It was only over time that I came to understand my dad's way of looking at things. I still could never be completely like him even if I tried, but I finally accepted that his was a one-track mind. And if you were to select a main focus for your life, God wasn't too bad of a choice.

* * *

We had been told by the Hospice folks that when it came time for Dad to die, he'd probably do it when there was nobody around. We made sure that wasn't going to happen. There was always at least one of us – and usually four or five – in his hospital room around the clock during his last three or four days. Two nights before he passed, I believed I was going to be the one who witnessed his final breath of this life.

45

It was my turn to spend the night in his room, and at one point his breathing became so sporadic that I thought for sure it was finally going to be over. But each time a long pause occurred, it was followed by a gasping breath before he settled into a regular pattern again. At one point when he seemed somewhat alert, I held his hand firmly and told him softly what a great father he had been through the years.

He hadn't opened his eyes for a day or two, but suddenly his eyelids lifted and he stared wide-eyed at me with what seemed like a hint of recognition. His eyes closed and I don't know if they ever opened again. But I kept talking to him much of that night and I hope he somehow sensed the love I was expressing.

Then, on Monday evening, with only my sister, Carol, by his side and the rest of us five minutes away eating dinner, he breathed his last. After fighting to stay alive for a week, he spent his final few moments on Earth alone with the daughter whose birth he had been unable to witness while he fought in World War II. Carol called us on her cellphone and we all jumped up from dessert and walked swiftly over to the hospital. No one said a word.

We entered his room and the first thing I noticed was Carol's tear-streaked face. Then I looked at Dad lying there, suddenly so peaceful after having experienced such labored breathing for so long. Mom dropped to her knees and started sobbing. Once we lifted her up, we all stood around the bed, holding his arms and hands, still warm to the touch.

* * *

Several years after Dad's departure to a much better place, Carol shared her thoughts with me about those final moments.

"Being with Dad when he died feels like such a gift... that he gave me something – I don't even have a word for it – almost sacred," she said. "It felt like a confirmation that all was well between us, having gotten past earlier struggles. That he felt safe to let go while I was there and to allow me the privilege of walking him home."

Right after someone dies, especially after a long illness, it's difficult to remove that picture of how they looked in their final days and weeks from your mind. Only time provides a fresh perspective and allows you to envision the person as he or she was in healthier times.

More than 17 years have passed since we buried Dad, and now other images have replaced the ones from his deathbed that stuck in my mind for so long… standing behind the backstop and shouting out encouragement to me when I was up to bat… putting his arm around me and praising me for a good grade in school or a nice play in the field… all bundled up and pulling a sled with four kids on it to church when the car wouldn't start. And, one that I hope will never leave my mind as long as I live – on his knees in his home office every single day, elbows on his chair and head buried in his hands, eyes closed and brow furrowed, praying for his family.

Now I have a family to live for and pray for. Now I can be ready when "Mr. Boyle" is asked to step up and deliver. Now I can respond in confidence, thanks to the legacy Dad left me.

Fifth Inning

The Friendly Confines

The secret plan had been in the works for several weeks. It was now simply a matter of waiting for Ernie Banks to hit his 499th career home run and then figuring out which particular day would work best for a junior ditch day involving a clandestine trip to Wrigley Field. Among the many factors we had to take into consideration for this stealth mission was the fact that a few of us were members of the high school varsity baseball team.

While we felt no qualms about missing a practice, we weren't willing to cut school on a game day to participate in this unauthorized pilgrimage merely for the off chance that Banks might make history with number 500. Compounding that sticky problem was the possibility of a last-minute high school make-up game being scheduled on the proposed ditch day.

So it was with much covert planning that we finally decided on Tuesday, May 12, 1970, for our venture to the Friendly Confines on Clark and Addison streets in Chicago. And like all schemes contrived by loud-mouthed teenagers, it did not remain a private matter for long. By the time Monday the 11th rolled around, there were nearly as many Wheaton North High School faculty and administration members who knew about the proposed ditch day as there were students.

The principal declared that juniors would serve detentions if they had an unexcused absence the following day, and one of our baseball coaches told the team in a hastily-called meeting that anybody who did not show up for Tuesday's after-school practice had better be in the hospital having a kidney transplant if he wanted to escape the severe consequences he had in mind.

This really put a damper on the carefully crafted proceedings, and most of the juniors who had considered going to Wrigley Field on Tuesday experienced a change of heart. A few of us, including two members of the team –Tom Wilson and me – figured we'd go ahead and take our punishment if necessary, while three other friends whose parents had no problem calling in sick for them said they'd join us. After all, there was a possibility that Ernie could launch the 500th home run of his glorious career on this day, and if that were to happen, we would have regretted not going for the rest of our lives.

My parents were in the dark about this escapade, and that's where I wanted them to stay. There was no way I was going to ask them to call in sick for me because I knew what the answer would be. I had learned long ago that integrity was one of my parents' highest priorities, and while they'd go to bat for me in a situation in which they believed I was in the right, they would not lie for me or for anybody else.

As planned, my ride dropped me off at Glenn Rudolph's house a few blocks from the Wheaton train station on Tuesday morning. Glenn, who had already gotten into some trouble at school that year, easily convinced his mom to call in sick for him. She figured if he didn't go to school, she wouldn't have to take a call from the principal that day regarding his behavior. Little did she know.

Here's where I made my big mistake. Instead of showing some honor and just calling the school Tuesday morning and telling them I was too well to attend, I asked Glenn to pose as my father and make the call for me. He phoned the school once I arrived at his house, but instead of the usual secretary answering, it was one of the school administrators on the other end of the line. Glenn became unnerved, and rather than immediately hanging up, said, "Hello, this is Mr. Boyle. Tim has the flu and won't be able to attend school today."

When the school official did not burst out laughing, it confirmed once and for all that he did not possess a sense of humor. Or a soul, for that matter. He'd had the distinct pleasure of several visits to his office from Glenn during the school year and knew his voice well. "That's very interesting, Glenn," he replied. "I'll be sure to let the real Mr. Boyle know about this."

"That didn't go real good," Glenn confessed to me after hanging up the phone. "I'm afraid they may be on to us." My goose was cooked at that point and I knew it. I thought about dashing off to school at that moment and telling the principal it was all a big mistake, but I really wanted to see the game and didn't want my friends thinking I was a coward.

So, "Mr. Boyle" and I headed over to the train station where we met our three friends and set off for our day in the sun. Or so we thought. The closer we got to Chicago, the darker the clouds appeared through the train windows. "Maybe it's because these windows are tinted," Glenn offered just before a thunderclap nearly knocked the train off its tracks.

By the time we walked six blocks from the Chicago train station to the elevated train, then another couple of blocks from the el to Wrigley Field, we were drenched. And the sky was still dark. And it was still raining. Tom and I looked at each other as if to say, "I can't believe we're going to get in serious trouble because we skipped school for a rainout." So, with no other options available, we all just wished really hard that it would stop raining.

And miraculously, our wish was granted. As noon approached, the rain stopped, the dark clouds obediently headed to the east and the sun began shining brightly. We went into the park at the bleachers entrance on the corner of Waveland and Sheffield avenues, walked up the long winding cement ramp and found plenty of room in the left-center field portion of the bleachers.

Drying off our seats with napkins, we settled in for a game against the Atlanta Braves. I was hoping against hope that Ernie Banks would come through with his 500th career homer and make it worth

50

whatever discipline awaited me both at school and home.

We didn't have to wait long. In the second inning, good old number 14, with his dancing fingers on the bat handle and right elbow held high, cocked his mighty wrists and stroked a pitch from Braves hurler Pat Jarvis on the line into the left field bleachers about 50 feet to our right. The ball bounced back onto the playing field as the small crowd erupted, and Ernie loped around the bases with elbows swinging high while Jack Brickhouse and other Cubs announcers ruptured their spleens screaming in celebration.

After jumping up and down for five minutes, we sat back down and watched the rest of the game. Can't remember who won. Didn't care too much then and don't care enough to look it up now. All I knew was that I had just witnessed my all-time favorite athlete's greatest milestone, and whatever heat was in store for me when I returned home was a small price to pay.

When we arrived back at Glenn's house late that afternoon, his mom informed us that a school administrator had called her at work to tell her about his fascinating conversation with "Tim's father." She also told me that the principal had called my mother and that I should be prepared for the worst when I got home.

To my surprise, my parents decided to play dumb and give me a chance to admit my sin before they brought it up and pronounced judgment. When I sat down for dinner, my mom nonchalantly asked me how school had gone that day. I just shrugged and said that it had probably been a typical school day. My dad then matter-of-factly inquired as to how baseball practice had gone, and I shrugged again and said that it had probably been a typical baseball practice. Because I knew that they knew, I was determined not to tell an outright lie as I probably would have if I hadn't known that they knew. Or something like that.

Following a long pause, I said, "Well, if you don't want to

discuss the subject, I certainly don't either," and then headed up to my bedroom. That probably wasn't the wisest tactic I could have employed. Both Mom and Dad came up to my room after a few minutes and calmly told me they knew what I had done that day. They also said that if I would have admitted it as soon as I came home, my punishment would not have been as severe as it now would be.

I believe they grounded me for a month, but that wasn't nearly as awful as what happened at school. In addition to serving a week's worth of detentions – I'm not sure, but I believe the principal also might have put us on double-secret probation – our baseball coaches forced Tom and me to field ground balls and flies from 7 to 8 a.m. for five consecutive days and suspended us for one game. We could dress for that next game, but they assured us we wouldn't play in it.

Nobody was going to miss my bat or glove because a senior started ahead of me at second base. But Tom was a starter and a good hitter, and his absence would be felt. Sure enough, it was a close game and at the very least we needed Tom as a pinch-hitter in the final inning. Deciding they'd rather try to win the game than stick with the sentencing, the coaches sent Tom up to pinch hit. I believe he popped up and we lost the game. I remember wanting so badly to say to one of the coaches, "What was our punishment supposed to be again?" But I was already in enough trouble. I was targeted for a starting role the following year, so I kept my mouth shut.

I was very lucky to have seen Ernie's 500th homer in person, which didn't surprise older brother Bill. He has always considered me one of the luckiest people on Earth. While it's true that good fortune seems to smile on me regarding things that don't really matter much, such as games between friends, I'm afraid it doesn't carry over to most life situations often enough. There was another time when I was right on the verge of experiencing a very lucky break at Wrigley Field, but would need an unusual play to make it happen.

I was in my early teens, sitting in the left field bleachers with some friends for a Cubs-Giants game. It was hot and we had been there since a couple of hours before the game even started. I think I was half-asleep when the Giants loaded the bases with one out. Third baseman Jim Ray Hart was at bat, and out of total boredom, I bet a 20-something Bleacher Bum in the row in front of me – complete with yellow helmet and blue bandana – that Hart would hit into a double play.

Now ordinarily, the shirtless, bronzed, beer-guzzling Bums would never lower themselves to speak with scrawny, stupid little kids like us. But prior to the start of the game we had impressed them with our baseball knowledge. We were also able to settle several of their arguments with the latest edition of *The Sporting News* that I carried with me everywhere I went. (By the way, I looked up the word "dork" recently in an online dictionary and saw an old picture of myself next to the word. Not to mention a new picture.)

I knew the odds of a twin killing were decent yet not great, but I also knew that Hart often hit the ball pretty hard, so I thought a quick 6-4-3 double play was definitely within the realm of possibility. I was working off a hunch, and since I had a little more cash in my wallet than usual that day, I decided to take a chance with some of it.

"Hey, if you want to throw $10 away, that's fine by me," growled the Bum, whose sweaty back my knees had inadvertently bumped against several times, soliciting an increasingly hostile series of glares.

After a few of my buddies and the Bums gave me quizzical looks, we shook hands on the bet. The Bums started chuckling between their hiccups, and when I turned in a hopeful fashion to my friends for support, I received something slightly different.

"You're a moron," one said.

"You're an idiot," another uttered.

"You do know there are runners on second and third, right?" one of my friends asked.

"Huh?"

Squinting toward first base from the left field bleachers some 380 feet away, I realized I had mistaken the Giants first base coach for a base runner, which made me think the bags were juiced. The likelihood of a double play occurring with runners on second and third was remote, to say the least.

I reluctantly fished in my wallet for a couple of $5 bills to place in the greedy palm of the conscienceless opportunistic brute in front of me. While the Bums loudly calculated how many beers they could score for $10 – which I believe was five back then – three Giants players did something for which I will always love them.

Cubs pitcher Ken Holtzman delivered a pitch that Hart hit on the ground to Ron Santo at third base. Willie McCovey, who was on third base, broke for home and Santo threw him out. Cubs catcher Randy Hundley then noticed Willie Mays straying too far off second base. He fired the ball to second baseman Glenn Beckert, who applied the tag for a highly unlikely but very real double play.

The crowd erupted, but nobody howled as loudly as my friends and me. The disgruntled Bleacher Bum shook his head slowly, scowled at me like he wanted to crush my head with Hart's bat, crumpled up a $10 bill and threw it at me in disgust before trudging off to the restroom. At that point, my friends and I decided that transferring to the right field bleachers for the rest of the game would be a prudent maneuver, so we sauntered on over with $10 now burning a hole in my pocket.

* * *

If you go to enough games – and I've probably been to about

250 of them at Wrigley Field through the years – you see a lot of interesting things. One of the highlights that stands out in my mind is a no-hitter by Cubs pitcher Burt Hooton against Philadelphia in 1972 in a steady, cold drizzle. There were fewer than 10,000 of us in the ballpark that day. Another is a bench-clearing brawl in 1987, sparked by an Eric Show fastball to the head of a red-hot Andre Dawson, who charged the mound after lying in the batter's box for several minutes. I was in the right field bleachers for both games.

One of the coolest games I ever went to – despite the fact that the team I was cheering for lost – was the 1962 All-Star Game at Wrigley Field. Actually, it was the second of two All-Star Games that year in an experiment that lasted only four seasons. The first thing I noticed when I entered the park that morning with brother Bill was the red, white and blue bunting you only see in ballparks on special occasions. Because the Cubs had never played in the World Series during my lifetime, this was a rare occurrence at Wrigley.

I was nine years old, so I don't remember too many details from that All-Star Game. One thing I do vividly recall was a line drive home run by Rocky Colavito of the Detroit Tigers that rocketed over the ivy-covered left field wall in about two seconds. Another was Ernie Banks hitting a triple – a rather unusual feat in a small park such as Wrigley – and scoring on a Billy Williams ground out.

Looking up the recap in an online archive, I see that the American League won 9-4 and that Pete Runnels of the Boston Red Sox, Leon "Daddy Wags" Wagner of the Los Angeles Angels and John Roseboro of the Los Angeles Dodgers also hit homers that day. The game was noteworthy for another reason – it was the last American League All-Star Game victory until 1971 and one of only two A.L. triumphs in the Mid-Summer Classic in a 23-year span beginning in 1960.

Two other games that filled me with opposite emotions also come to mind. As an eighth grader, I went with brother Bill to a Cubs-

55

Reds game and we again sat in the right field bleachers. All week I'd been anticipating seeing Ernie Banks in action, but in the fourth inning Pete Rose spiked the Cubs first baseman on the foot while trying to beat out a grounder to shortstop and Ernie had to leave the game. I remember the bleacher creatures, in obviously less politically correct times, repeatedly chanting, "Rose is a fairy" when he took his left field position a few minutes later.

The antithesis of that game for me was a mid-September contest on a Friday afternoon in 1984. The Cubs were leading the National League East Division by 7½ games, but the New York Mets were in town, hoping to cut their deficit to 4½ with a weekend series sweep. Every Cubs fan was thinking back to the big choke in 1969, and the doomsday prophets were predicting a repeat.

The Cubs were leading 3-0 in the bottom of the sixth inning on a chilly day at Wrigley in the first game of the series. With two outs and Cubs runners on second and third, the Mets decided to issue an intentional walk to Ron Cey, filling the bases for slow-footed Jody Davis.

Once the first intentional ball was thrown to Cey, it was as if the crowd had been orchestrated to respond. Everybody in the park, it seemed, stood and started chanting, "JO-DY, JO-DY, JO-DY, JO-DY." It was a major uproar that just kept getting louder as the Cubs catcher approached the plate. On the first pitch, Davis drilled a shot to left-center field that carried into the third or fourth row of the bleachers for a grand slam.

The place went absolutely nuts. It was like the Cubs had just won the World Series. People who had never met were hugging each other and everybody was jumping up and down and shrieking at the top of their lungs. I think it was then that we all realized the Cubs were headed for the postseason for the first time since 1945.

Speaking of the playoffs – and Cubs fans who are alive today

56

haven't had many opportunities to do that – another magical moment occurred at a game I attended at Wrigley Field. Chicago trailed the Florida Marlins by two runs heading into the bottom of the ninth inning in Game 1 of the 2003 National League Championship Series.

The Marlins had taken an 8-6 lead with a pair of runs in the top of the frame, but the Cubs put a man on second base. With two outs and two strikes, free-swinging Sammy Sosa crushed a home run onto Waveland Avenue to tie it, and the crescendo was ear-splitting. Unfortunately, the Cubs lost the game in the 11th inning and eventually blew a three games-to-one lead and the series. (More on this tragic event later.)

You know what always makes me really jealous for some reason? It's when people rattle off the exorbitant number of major league baseball parks they've been to. I suppose it's because baseball stadiums are all so different and each one offers a unique experience and, well, doggone it, I just wish I could visit more of them. In addition to Wrigley Field, Miller Park in Milwaukee, and both the old Comiskey Park and U.S. Cellular Field in Chicago, I've seen games at only seven other ballparks.

Four of those arenas – Fenway Park in Boston, Camden Yards in Baltimore, Candlestick Park in San Francisco and Busch Stadium in St. Louis – I was able to visit due to being in town on business. I also went to Dodger Stadium in Los Angeles on several occasions while visiting sister Carol and brother Dave, and took in a Cubs-Phillies game with the family at old Connie Mack Stadium in Philadelphia on our way to New Jersey one summer.

One of my most interesting excursions to a ballpark outside of Chicago occurred in 1964. The family was once again on the way to Cape May, New Jersey for a vacation (I can't remember going on vacation anywhere else for the first 18 years of my life), but first we stopped off at a quaint little place called New York City to attend the World's Fair.

With six of us wanting to do six different things and most of us complaining about the heat and having to walk so much, by late afternoon my dad was ready to trade us all in for a family to be named later. Topping it off, we tried eating dinner at an outdoor steak house that I'm pretty sure established a Guinness World Record for the most flies landing on food in 30 minutes.

Completely disgusted, my father announced that he was heading over to a baseball game at nearby Shea Stadium. Those who wanted to join him were welcome if they promised not to moan about anything for the next several hours. Those who weren't interested could either stay at the Fair or return to our hotel.

Bill and I went with Dad, while Mom, Carol and seven-year-old Dave stayed at the Fair. I believe the Mets beat the San Francisco Giants that evening, and I'm certain it was the strangest atmosphere I have ever encountered for a major league baseball game. The place was a zoo, and the crowd seemed better suited for a circus than a ballgame.

What I didn't fully comprehend as an 11-year-old was that Mets fans had long since given up on their team being competitive and had decided they might as well have as much fun as possible while occasionally glancing at the field to watch the team create new ways to lose. By the time we visited Shea Stadium in mid-summer, the Mets were well on the way to their third of four consecutive seasons with at least 109 losses after joining the National League in 1962.

Managed by the one and only Casey Stengel, this was a squad that couldn't pitch, hit or field. By season's end, the '64 Mets would give up more runs than any other National League team while scoring fewer than all but one club. There were many hilarious things happening on the field in those days, but the fans did their best to match the players in zaniness. When spectators weren't running onto the field, they were holding up bizarre signs or screaming crazy slogans. The only thing louder than these crowds was the deafening roar of jets flying overhead every five minutes in and out of LaGuardia Airport.

At the game we attended, kids conducted a contest to determine who could slide the farthest down a grandstand railing without falling off. It was so entertaining that every fan within three sections stood and watched. They would cheer vigorously when one child made it all the way down 40 rows of seats, laugh when a kid fell off the railing into the aisle or onto a fan's lap around the halfway mark and boo when a youngster failed to slide past the first few rows.

* * *

There are many people who have attended hundreds of major league baseball games without ever coming away with a souvenir. I've been fortunate enough to snag three baseballs at games through the years, and older brother Bill caught one using my mitt. In 1962, Bill and I were in the left field bleachers at Wrigley Field watching outfielders shag flies during the pregame practice and hoping one would sail beyond their reach.

Bill, who did not take his glove to the game, told me we'd have a better chance of getting a souvenir if he used my glove, and I reluctantly agreed. Sure enough, Cubs pitcher Glen Hobbie got too much wood on a ball he had tossed in the air and whacked toward the outfielders. Suddenly we were surrounded by a mass of humanity as the sphere zeroed in on us. Bill stuck my glove up – in the midst of about a dozen other mitts – and somehow came down with it. I never would have been able to reach high enough to catch that ball.

When we got off the train at the College Avenue stop in Wheaton late that afternoon, Bill and I tossed the ball back and forth to each other as we climbed the steep hill on Stoddard Avenue. I was wearing my glove at that point and he was catching the ball barehanded. We vowed that we would not let that special baseball touch the ground during the entire three-block walk, and while we had some close calls, we met our goal. We felt like victorious warriors returning from the battle as we marched into our house on East Jefferson Avenue and proudly showed our parents the ball.

59

One of the three baseballs I ended up garnering solo was a breeze, another resulted from a freaky bounce and the last one I had to work for. The easy one came when I was in my mid-30s. I was vacationing in Palm Springs, California and I arrived early for a spring training game between the Cubs and Angels. I was hanging out in the left field corner with a couple of guys I didn't know when some slugger drilled a batting practice rocket over our heads. It slammed against a wall in foul territory and ricocheted back toward us. I outran my competitors to the baseball and scooped it up easily.

A few years later, I was at a Cubs-Cardinals game at Wrigley Field with my twin nephews. We were sitting between home plate and third base, about 25 rows back. On the third pitch of the game, leadoff hitter Ozzie Smith fouled off a pitch that flew over our heads to the left, slammed against the façade separating the upper and lower decks, and landed about five rows in front of us before skittering underneath the seats and coming to rest right in front of me.

I quickly reached down and grabbed it – one of my nephews tells me I muscled him out of the way – and before the first out of the game had been recorded, I had a souvenir. Suddenly it dawned on me that my nephew might be experiencing a feeling similar to the one that ripped me apart when I was the kid who narrowly missed grabbing a foul ball off the bat of Richie Ashburn that lay near my feet.

Why didn't I let him grab it? I asked myself. It was too late to do anything about that, but I told the boys that the baseball was theirs to share. To this day, that ball is still on display at their mom's home in Arlington Heights, Illinois.

My proudest moment in terms of snaring a baseball at a game came during the 1988 season. I was sitting halfway between third base and the left field wall at Wrigley Field, about 10 rows deep. Keith Moreland, who had been one of my favorite players when he wore a Cubs uniform but was now a member of the San Diego Padres, smoked a line drive that kept hooking toward my boss and me.

I had my baseball glove with me that day – much to my boss' embarrassment – so I stepped into the aisle, moved a few feet to my left and leaped to make the catch. The ball was hit pretty hard, and I really felt it on the palm of my hand, but didn't let on that I was in pain.

Gloveless fans in the line of fire were very grateful that a 35-year-old with a baseball glove had reached up to catch a line drive that could have killed someone. A number of spectators gave me a rousing cheer for making the grab. I waved my glove to acknowledge the brief ovation, then sat down and realized I had just enjoyed my 15 seconds of fame.

After the applause died down, a guy sitting several sections closer to home plate than I was screamed out "Boyle." I stood up again and saw a friend from my boyhood church in Wheaton. I had no idea he was at the game until then. Although I walked over to talk to him between innings, I didn't want to overdo it because I knew he had become a Padres fan in 1984 for the specific purpose of rooting against the Cubs in the playoffs. It's just not right to fraternize too much with the opposition.

* * *

The late, great Ernie Banks will never again hit a home run at Wrigley Field. Randy Hundley will never throw out another runner at second base. Burt Hooton will never toss another no-hitter. And Jody Davis will never propel the Cubs to another division title with a clutch grand slam. But there are plenty of other magical moments predestined for the Friendly Confines over the next couple of decades, and I'm determined to experience the pure pleasure of witnessing some of them in person.

Sixth Inning

Talking Heads, Talking Trash, Talking Dog

If you're ever my partner in a baseball trivia contest, I hope you know a lot of stuff that happened in the early to mid-1970s. Because I sure don't. I had been a pretty active jock in high school, even though I wasn't a particularly talented athlete. When I wasn't playing sports, I was watching or listening to games, or playing sports board games at home. In other words, I was a total geek for about as long as I could possibly be without committing permanent social suicide.

When I got away from the direct influence of my parents at age 19 in 1972 and began attending Northern Illinois University in DeKalb, I started hanging out with people who were far more interested in rock 'n' roll and that whole lifestyle than in sports. So, I put baseball and every other sport on the back burner for a while.

I won't embarrass my family with a litany of my activities during those college years. Suffice it to say that I did pretty much what most young adults were doing on secular college campuses during the early 1970s. Sports in general and baseball in particular had been such a big part of my life up until that time, but I really don't remember missing sports at all while living in DeKalb.

Music was one of my main substitutions for sports. I had enjoyed pop music for my first two years of high school before "graduating" to heavier bands such as Led Zeppelin in my junior and senior years. In college, I spent countless hours listening to the likes of David Bowie, Lou Reed, Todd Rundgren, Genesis (with Peter Gabriel), the Kinks and many others. Eventually I would get into what was then called the New Wave scene, enjoying Talking Heads, Elvis Costello, the Psychedelic Furs, Blondie and many others in that genre.

62

While living back home in Wheaton for a year between my sophomore and junior years of college, I even played bass in a band for a while. This despite an inability to read music, knowing nothing about the instrument and being basically tone deaf. Yeah, that's what you want in a bass player. The guitarist, drummer and keyboardist were friends, and they were looking for someone who would play bass adequately, keep his mouth shut and not try to take charge. I couldn't have taken charge even if I wanted to. They sold me a used Guild bass for $50 and taught me the absolute minimum I needed to know in order to play their songs.

Remarkably, we actually played a few shows in front of real people. Real bored people, but so what? One appearance for our band was scheduled for a Saturday in 1973 near Western Illinois University in Macomb, about a four-hour drive from where we all lived. High school friend and now WIU student Glenn Rudolph organized this huge event at Argyle Lake State Park, featuring nine or ten bands.

The night before the gig, we learned that 40,000-plus people were expected to attend. I was sweating bullets. Even if I had felt competent on the bass, I would have been very nervous. But the fact that I was so inexperienced caused me much trepidation. To be totally honest, I couldn't even properly tune my bass. After every two or three songs, the guitar player or drummer had to do it for me. How embarrassing is that?

What I was most afraid of on that particular occasion was that my fellow band members would start improvising at some point, and I would be clueless regarding what to do in front of thousands of people. The only thing I had going for me was the look – wavy brown hair that reached close to halfway down my back, a red satin shirt, bellbottoms and platform shoes. For that time, I looked a lot better than I sounded.

I had considerable trouble sleeping that night, and when I got out of bed at 5:30 in the morning and walked into the living room, there was already a group of people partying in anticipation of the day's

63

activities. Or perhaps they hadn't gone to bed the night before, I'm not sure. As it turned out, it didn't matter. Torrential downpours that began the previous evening continued throughout the day and washed out the show. Part of me was sad, but another part was relieved.

By the way, our band's name was "Wisdom" (not to be confused with a more recent metal band from Budapest), although my presence in the group made that moniker a bit of an oxymoron. One of the band members was envisioning a cover for our second album that would feature a rotten wisdom tooth. I guess the album title was going to be "Wisdom Twooth." Due to the fact that we never had a first record, putting out a follow-up album was definitely out of the question. While my band mates went on to achieve various levels of musical success, I ended up selling my bass when I needed cash. So much for my musical career.

My general nervousness for much of my adolescence and young adulthood was not limited to playing the bass. It began when I was a child and was a frequent occurrence. The common denominator was performance. I guess that's why they call it performance anxiety. Literally from as early as I can remember, I had problems in this area. Anytime I was about to do anything that would be observed by others, I experienced something between vague discomfort to raving paranoia. No matter what I was expected to do, from something as simple as saying a quick prayer at the dinner table to telling the class about my science project, I was absolutely convinced I was going to mess it up and be the target of mockery.

Some time ago, my older brother told me that he was probably the cause of my anxiety, due to his incessant badgering of me when we were kids. That might have been a factor, but obviously I was predisposed to this condition or it would not have affected me as dramatically as it did. In finally putting a label on it when I was in junior high school, our family doctor told me that I had an overactive nervous system and prescribed Valium. In my clinical opinion, I was just screwed up.

64

Here's an example. If I had a Little League game scheduled for 6:30 p.m., I'd start getting sweaty palms after lunch... three days earlier. I was a halfway decent ballplayer as a kid and really had no legitimate reason to worry – in almost every game, some other kid would strike out four times and let a fly ball bounce off his head – but I would work myself into such a state of nervousness that I had to engage in deep breathing exercises just to calm down... all over a Little League game nobody would even remember the next day.

Once the game started, I was usually OK because I was able to get rid of most of my nervous energy by running around. So the real problem was anticipation, and in particular a deep-rooted dread that I would make a huge mistake that would be witnessed by a group of people. The fact that a worse case scenario never played out for me on a ball field didn't keep me from figuring it was always lurking right around the next corner.

I did, however, experience a number of extremely humiliating moments away from the baseball diamond that fed my anxiety issues. One occurred at about age 10. My piano instructor was also our Sunday school teacher. He kept trying to convince me that I was ready to play a solo in front of the other kids at church without any sheet music, and I kept telling him I couldn't do it. In reality, I knew that song forward and backward, and could have played it in my sleep. But I didn't want to set myself up for possible failure. Finally, he talked to my parents about it and they insisted.

I hadn't been able to make my teacher believe I would choke when the pressure was on, but apparently I succeeded in convincing myself. When I sat down at the piano to play that simple song in front of my peers, my mind went blank. For the life of me, I could not remember the first key to strike and couldn't "hear" the song in my mind. After a couple of humiliating minutes trying to figure it out, my teacher gently rested his hand on my shoulder and said, "That's OK, Tim. We'll try it again some other time."

Uh, let me think for a minute… NO WE WON'T!!! With my tail between my legs, I crept back to my chair amid a deafening silence and stayed there for a minute or two until feeling sick to my stomach. Fortunately, I made it to the restroom before another disaster occurred, and this time I performed quite admirably.

* * *

I've probably been more nervous at some point over the past 50-plus years than I was as a nine-year-old prior to our Little League All-Star Game at Northside Park in Wheaton, Illinois. But I certainly can't remember when. I don't even know why I was selected for the team. They must have really needed a second baseman because I had a very average season in my first year in the league. I wasn't too much of a hitter, but I might have impressed somebody with my glove.

Why they had me leading off was just as much of a mystery. And because we were the visiting team, I was the first batter of the game. *Why me?* I thought. My fears were intensified when I looked out at the mound and saw who was warming up. Don Simmons was a tall, solidly-built, dark-complexioned left-hander who at age nine already had all the major league mannerisms down pat. He'd kick the rubber as if it had stolen his lunch money, throw down the rosin bag hard enough to form a crater in the mound and glare at the batter like he wanted to kill him. And he'd talk trash way before it was cool to trash talk.

Don was a natural choice as the starting pitcher for his league because he had mowed everybody down all season, including me. But it didn't hurt that his dad was his All-Star team's coach. In addition to possessing what seemed at the time like a blazing fastball, Don was just wild enough to make a hitter hesitant to dig in at the plate. He had hit a few batters during the season, and they were still probably feeling the pain.

For added effect, Don's hat flew off on nearly every pitch, and on windy days one of his infielders would have to retrieve it for him.

66

Instead of a "Thanks, buddy," Don would rip the cap out of his infielder's hand, grunt loudly and stomp back to the mound to resume his personal vendetta against batters. And when the umpire was preoccupied, he'd say something to the hitter along the lines of, "Do you want to walk back to your dugout now, or just wait until after I strike you out?"

My goal as I timidly slipped into the right-handed batter's box on that mid-summer day was to not whiff. Even a weak infield grounder would do the trick. I just didn't want to embarrass myself too badly. Especially with my dad behind me, his face pressed up against the backstop and the familiar, "Be ready, Tim" ringing in my ears. I was ready, all right. Ready to strike out and slink back to the dugout.

I often let the first pitch go by when I was the leadoff hitter in a game. Back then, a lot of leadoff hitters did that. Getting on base and moving base runners along was considered more important in those days than it is today. But something told me to take a whack at the first pitch if it looked hittable.

Don wound up in his typical windmill fashion and let loose with a fastball that appeared to be headed directly down the middle of the plate. Knowing the pitch that was released from less than 45 feet away would be on top of me in an instant, I started to swing my bat as soon as he let go of the ball, just as my father had taught me. I could always check my swing if it looked like the pitch would be out of the strike zone.

It wasn't and I didn't. I teed off on that pitch – well, at least as powerfully as a scrawny nine-year-old can – and the solid crack of the bat against the ball resounded loudly. I'd love to report that I sent the baseball soaring over the left field fence, jogged around the bases while the crowd gave me a standing ovation and was mobbed at home plate by my awed teammates. Alas, that didn't occur.

But I did smack a line drive directly over second base that

reached the center fielder on a few hops as I scurried to first base with a single. The parents of my teammates were too stunned to cheer, so I clearly heard my proud father bellow, "That-a-boy, Timmy!" Once I settled in at first base, I glanced at Don, who was angrily staring a hole right through me. *How dare a little punk like you get a hit off me on the first pitch of the game?!?* he seemed to be thinking. Easily intimidated, I might have considered apologizing.

I'm sure Don's dad would have preferred that his son start the game with a strikeout, but he was always on the lookout for somebody who could help his team the following year. I don't know what strings Mr. Simmons pulled, but the next season I was moved to his team and found myself a teammate of Don's. I'll tell you, it was a lot more fun playing second base with him pitching than trying to hit his fastball… even if it meant getting his hat ripped out of my hands when I'd retrieve it for him. Don and I were teammates for the next three years in Little League, and we won two league championships with him on the hill.

* * *

I've always been an animal lover. The first dog I remember us having was Skippy, but I'm pretty sure we were forced to put him down after he bit one of our obnoxious neighbors in Oak Park. I never asked my parents or older siblings about that. I guess I just don't want to know.

When we moved from Oak Park to Wheaton at age eight, the movers found a kitten and asked if we wanted him. My dad said "no" and my sister said "yes." Because my sister was upset about leaving all her high school friends in Oak Park, Mom decided we would keep him. We named him "Tiger," and I think a real tiger would have been a better pet. This cat was wild, and he never settled down. He bit at least one of us every day for a couple of months, jumped up on the dining room table regularly to drink out of our water glasses and tore up every piece of clothing and bedding he could get his clawed paws on.

I was so infuriated with this cat that one day I decided to turn the tables on him and bite him. (Did I mention that I was not a particularly bright kid? Not necessary at this point, I guess.) All I got out of the deal was a mouthful of fur and a strange look from Tiger. On the plus side, the feline stayed away from me for a while. Eventually my parents got rid of him too, although I don't know how. Again, I've never asked. Sometimes it's just better not to know things.

Soon after, we got a puppy from a kid on my Little League team. Prince was half-cocker spaniel and half-setter. He was the size of a large cocker spaniel and had the handsome reddish-brown coat of a setter, with white spots here and there including the bridge of his nose. He wasn't a genius – although he did talk once – but he understood most of what we told him and learned a few tricks. Most important, he was a great companion for me as I tried to adjust to a new neighborhood, new school and new friends. Simultaneously I was mourning the loss of my old neighborhood, school and friends, so his presence was a big help to me during the challenging transition.

Prince lived a long time, despite us almost losing him once. Actually, *I* almost lost him. I was a junior in college, so Prince must have been 12 years old by then, and he was still pretty sprightly for his age. When my parents were about to go on vacation, they allowed me to take care of him in DeKalb for a week rather than putting him in a kennel. The first day I had him, he found a way to escape from our house and couldn't be found anywhere.

I was so scared that Prince was going to get hit by a car or found by jerks who might abuse him. My roommates and I spent an entire day looking for him, to no avail. Finally that evening, I got a call from my parents – who hadn't even left for vacation yet – saying they'd received a call from a DeKalb resident who'd found Prince and called the number on his tag. My parents already thought I was an irresponsible slacker, and this did nothing to help my cause. But I was so elated my dog was safe and sound that their displeasure with me was easy to accept.

69

I drove quickly to the house where my dog was – clear across town – and hugged him like I'd never hugged him before. Prince only lived two or three more years before suffering a stroke. We had to put him to sleep, and to this day it's one of the saddest moments of my life. I've had a few dogs since him and loved every one of them dearly, but nothing could ever top my feelings for Prince. So much more than a dog, he was my friend at a time when I really needed one. If you're an animal lover, you know exactly what I mean.

Oh, yeah, about him talking. Prince was eight years old and I was a junior in high school. My daily routine on school days was to take him for a walk right before breakfast. On this particular day, he was in my bedroom waiting for me to get dressed and attach the leash to his collar. For some reason, he seemed more excited than usual to get outside and start tugging. At one point while I was pulling a shirt over my head, Prince let out a long, drawn-out, high-pitched yawn that through some bizarre coincidence sounded exactly like someone saying, "Let's go!" I was freaked. I could barely move. I just stared at him, wondering if he were possessed or something.

Had I been alone in the house with Prince that morning, I'm sure I would have later told disbelieving family members what happened and then forgotten about it in a few days. But what has kept this legendary story alive in our family for well over four decades is the fact that my mom heard it. A few seconds after Prince "spoke," Mom came rushing into my room from the kitchen and asked in a startled voice, "Who said that?!?!" She knew I was incapable of speaking in that strange voice, and she was as wigged-out about it as I was.

All I could do was point to Prince. "No!" my mom exclaimed. "Yes!" I replied. Prince must have thought we were idiots. At least his sentence contained more than one word. For the next few days, I had a number of one-on-one powwows with my dog regarding the incident.

"OK, I know now that you can talk," I'd tell him. "Your cover is blown. So let's just talk. It'll be our little secret. Nobody else has to know. It's OK, you can talk only to me the way Mister Ed talks only to Wilbur." But it never happened again. Not even close.

I'm one of those poor saps who believes animals we've known on Earth will be in Heaven someday, at least if we want them to be. (There might be a different eternal destination in store for Tiger.) I realize there's no biblical basis for this argument, but I just have a hunch it's true. If so, maybe they'll be able to talk. Hey, a serpent talked in the Garden of Eden and neither Eve nor Adam seemed too surprised by it. Of course, the snake probably said something more along the lines of "Let's eat" than "Let's go," but the principle is the same.

If our former pets are in Heaven with us and if they can talk, Prince will tell me all about his adventure of roaming around the streets and fields of DeKalb that day and whether he was really speaking to me that morning in Wheaton. Those are the first two things I'll ask him about... after giving him a hug that will put all my previous earthly hugs to shame.

Seventh Inning

Games People Play

Inside baseball.

People today don't bat an eyelash when they hear that phrase. After all, seven major league teams currently play their games at ballparks with a retractable roof or a fixed roof. But back in 1965, when the then-Houston Colt .45s moved from Colt Stadium to the newly-opened Astrodome – changing their nickname to the Astros and becoming the first team in big league history to play their home games indoors – it was big news.

Many baseball purists were appalled at taking nature's elements out of play, but the novelty of the idea kept protest to a minimum. And anyone who has spent more than five minutes hanging out in Houston in the summer understands the desire to avoid that oppressive heat and humidity.

Growing up in the Midwest meant you could play baseball outdoors for only about seven months of the year. Unless, of course, you were willing to deal with frostbite, which could put a real damper on trying to grasp the seams of a baseball. March is usually too cold and wet, and in November it starts getting very chilly again. So, April through October – corresponding perfectly with the major league baseball season – is your window of opportunity.

This limited engagement has never been great news for Midwest kids, but it certainly worked out nicely for the manufacturers of baseball board games during the 1950s and '60s. They were well aware of the withdrawal pains suffered by true baseball fanatics during the off-season and fully understood that these addicted fans needed an outlet for the obsession to be involved in their sport in some fashion or

72

another year-round. And game creators knew that these kids – and some adults – were likely to roll the dice and spin the spinners by the warmth of a fireplace when it was too frigid or too dark to play outdoors.

Of course, that was then and this is now. Just try to persuade a child over the age of 5 to be involved in a board game today. To them, there's no difference between "board" and "bored." If it's not a fast-paced video game in which you can register 1,000 "kills" per minute and send blood flying in every direction, they're just not interested.

Both of my sons were much more skilled than I was at video games back in the day, including Lord of the Rings and Star Wars Galaxies – we didn't let them play the gruesome ones – but every once in a while I would convince one of them to join me in a baseball, football, basketball, hockey or golf video game. In those games, I could usually reach their talent level after a while. When I was really feeling my oats, I would make the mistake of taking a commanding lead in a baseball game. Invariably their interest level would plummet and the game would quickly degenerate into a bean ball war.

One of my sister's old boyfriends used to drop by our house in Wheaton, Illinois regularly to pick her up for dates during the summers of their college years in the early 1960s. He told me some time later that almost every time he entered our home, the first sound he heard was the vigorous rattling of dice in the plastic shakers we used for our APBA baseball board game.

For those of you unfamiliar with the game – perhaps you have played similar games such as Strat-O-Matic at some point – APBA features a 2½-inch by 3½-inch card for every major league baseball player, plus playing boards and dice. The player cards come in team packets, and you can pit team against team or make up your own all-star squads and let them duke it out.

The cards feature vertical rows of numbers. Once you've rolled the dice, you match up the dice roll with the corresponding number on

73

the card, then refer to the large playing boards for the result. Each card is computer programmed so that the player will generally perform as he would in real life, based on his statistics from the previous season.

Of course, almost anything can happen in an individual game and even during a single short season, depending on the dice rolls. But over the course of a longer season, a slugger such as Mike Trout can be expected to hit considerably more home runs than most players, Miguel Cabrera will compile a higher than normal batting average, Jon Lester will rack up plenty of wins, etc.

The beauty of APBA baseball is that you can play a complete game in 30 minutes or fewer. That's due to the very wise elimination of virtually all the pitches that in a real game would result in a ball or strike. Almost every dice roll produces an end result – walk, strikeout, fly out, hit, etc. – speeding up the process immensely. You even get the quirky stuff with APBA, such as player injuries, ejections and rainouts. And this game is just as fun playing solo as it is against a friend… or an enemy, for that matter.

So, for a kid in the Fifties and Sixties with an insatiable appetite for baseball and a lot of time to kill, APBA was the perfect outlet. From age eight until about 15, I played entire seasons with these cards, keeping a detailed box score for every game and concluding with the World Series (there were no playoffs prior to 1969). I'd even throw in an All-Star Game or two for the fun of it.

Brother Dave would conduct his own APBA league simultaneously, as would other friends of ours, and I can't begin to tell you how much time we spent informing each other about which teams were in first place in our leagues, which power hitters were leading the way in home runs and which pitchers were crafting the lowest ERA's.

Depending on the rolls of the dice in our various homes in the neighborhood, Stan Musial might be batting .500 in one league and .186 in another, while Sam McDowell could be posting his 10th victory in one league and struggling to earn his third "W" in another. All of which led to intellectual conversations between us geeks, such as:

"Norm Cash stinks!"

"Are you kidding me? He's great!"

"What are you talking about? He strikes out every other time up and hasn't hit a homer since the opener."

"Obviously you can't roll dice very well. He has six homers in his first 10 games in my league. What I don't understand is why Sandy Koufax can't get anybody out."

"You're crazy. Koufax blows everybody away. He's already 5-0 with a 1.76 earned run average in my league."

And so on and so forth. APBA is still around and going strong, thanks in large part, I would imagine, to older gamers. From the mid-1980s to the mid-1990s, I revisited the game and played in a league with some friends for several months each year. We used the old dice and board game, but many people have advanced to the computer game.

I've played the game on computer, and several others like it, but I just can't get the impression out of my mind that I've lost some control by pushing a button on the keyboard to initiate a play rather than rattling that narrow, yellow, plastic shaker and rolling the big red die and the little white die onto a table. That hands-on experience makes you feel as if you are influencing the result in some fashion, and I swear that every once in a great while you can actually "will" the dice to land how you want them to if you focus hard enough.

Even some of the hardcore fans who go to the company's conventions might not know that the APBA baseball game evolved from a game called National Pastime. The only reason I know this is because my dad used to play it in the 1930s. Unfortunately, he didn't keep his old player cards or boards, but I still have a bunch of his notebooks in which he recorded box scores of the countless games he played.

His handwriting was meticulous, and I can recreate almost every game he played just by looking at his notations for each hitter. He was using player cards with the names of legends such as Babe Ruth, Hack Wilson, Lefty Grove and Carl Hubbell inscribed on them, and I can only guess how my dad must have felt when a dice roll resulted in a hero of his such as Al Simmons tearing into a pitch for a game-winning hit.

After he finished a game, Dad would add up every batter's at-bats, runs, hits, RBI, putouts, assists and errors, as well as every pitcher's innings, runs, earned runs, hits, strikeouts and walks. (I guess that's what happens when you're an introvert with no brothers.) In 1961, Dad saw an advertisement in a sports magazine for the APBA baseball game and, recognizing it as being nearly identical to the one he'd played as a boy, bought it for my brothers and me. It wasn't long before we were hooked.

Speaking of my dad and games, he actually invented a baseball game called "Inside Baseball" while serving in World War II. He had it professionally designed before producing a couple of prototypes with testimonials written on the box by major leaguers such as Birdie Tebbetts and George Earnshaw, who he met during the war. But he was unable to sell it to a game company when he returned to the States.

There are two decks of cards in Dad's game – a red one for the team in the field and a blue one for the team at bat. Each of the pitcher's cards features either a "Ball" or "Strike" designation, as well as two or three colors within a circle in both the top left and bottom right corners of the card, plus a result. Each of the batter's cards includes a one-color circle in both the top left and bottom right corners, as well as a number of results for different situations.

After shuffling the cards to begin an inning, each player draws six cards to use for that particular at-bat. Without showing opponents their cards, both players select one to use for the first pitch and throw them down simultaneously. The pitcher card always lands face up, while the batter has the option of taking the pitch by putting his card face down or swinging at the offering by placing it face up.

If the batter takes the pitch, the result is either a strike or a ball, depending on the pitcher card. When the batter swings at the pitch, he hits it only if the color on his card matches one of the colors on the pitcher's card. If the color does not match up, it's a strike; if it does match up, you look at the result on the pitcher's card.

Connecting with a "Ball" card generally results in a ground ball or pop up to an infielder or a fly ball to an outfielder. The pitcher then picks up a card from the top of the deck to determine the result of that play. If you connect with a "Strike" card, you hit a single, double, triple or homer. Once a batter makes an out or reaches a base, both players discard those six cards and draw six new ones.

One of the downsides to this game is that because the batter can't see the pitch coming, it's total guesswork regarding his choice to take the pitch or swing at it. Both batters and pitches are wise to "mix it up." If you become known as a first-pitch swinger, the pitcher will feed you only "Balls" on that first pitch, whereas if your habit as a pitcher is to consistently try to get ahead in the count, the batter will know to take a hack at the first pitch.

There are also options for the batter to try to steal a base or hit-and-run, while the pitcher can try to pick a runner off a base. Because it's a pitch-by-pitch affair, a typical game lasts at least an hour and a half. Back in the 1960s, it felt very cool to show friends a game my dad created, and I still have one of the only two copies of the game that ever existed.

Because baseball board games were popular in that era, there were plenty from which to choose. One of our favorites was All Star

Baseball. This game featured cutout cards of then-current stars and Hall of Famers, and when it was a particular player's turn at bat, we'd place his card over the center of the spinner device.

Then we'd give the spinner a whirl and see where the arrow ended up pointing. The best power hitters would contain the biggest spaces on their cards for numbers that corresponded to homers, doubles, etc., while the high on-base percentage batters would possess large spaces on their cards for numbers indicating singles and walks. You could play this game by yourself if you wanted to, but it was more fun squaring off against someone else, if for no other reason than there would be at least several instances in every game in which heated debate would arise regarding where the spinner had stopped.

"It's on the line," one of us whose batter was at the plate would shout, seeking a re-spin when clearly the arrow was leaning toward a number that corresponded to a rally-killing double play.

"On the line, my butt," the other would respond angrily, having already grabbed his leadoff hitter's card for the next inning and placed it on his spinner pad.

The APBA baseball board game may not have been high-tech back in the Sixties, but All Star Baseball was even less so, due to the many spins that were left open to interpretation by flagrantly biased young boys to whom losing was completely unacceptable.

There were times when disagreements became so intense that one of us would rip his opponent's card off the spinner, effectively ending that player's career. (Scotch taping these guys back together was a real challenge, and the spinner would often catch on the tape and hamper the spin.) The pair of combatants would continue their screaming match all the way to the door, vowing to never speak to each other as long as they lived. The next day, all was forgiven and forgotten.

Baseball was hardly the only indoor game we played. There were also plenty of football, basketball and hockey games that resulted in endless hours of fun for kids who were prisoners of their homes during Midwestern winters. One of the football games we played was the electronic game in which each player is manually stationed by his "coach" in a particular spot on the playing field. A tiny, oval-shaped piece of fabric represented the football, which you'd tuck into the arm of the quarterback or halfback.

In the old version of the game, after spending about five hours setting up a play, you'd flip the on-switch and the 10 seconds of fun would begin. First you'd hear a low-pitched, electronic hum and then you'd watch the little plastic and metal players move slowly on the 18-inch by 30-inch vibrating playing field. Offensive linemen would attempt to push defensive linemen out of the way while the ball carrier tried to make his way up field before being touched by a defender.

The most bizarre element of this game back then was the forward pass, for which you'd utilize something that can only be described as a mini-catapult. You'd try to launch the ball in the vicinity of an end who had moved downfield as quickly as possible, even though the odds were about one in a billion that you'd come close. The same instrument was used for field goal kicks and extra point attempts, but it was so difficult to aim accurately that you were just as likely to send the "ball" hurtling toward the sideline as you were to steer it near the goal post. On the plus side, if you did mange to "kick" it straight toward the goal post, a 90-yard field goal was very possible.

There were a few other indoor football games we would play, but only one basketball game. This was the game that utilized a ping-pong ball that rolled around the sloping court until settling into one of the 10 holes (five per team), each representing a player. If the ball fell into one of your holes, you had the option of trying to pass it to one of the holes closer to the basket in order to set up a higher percentage shot, or just fire away at the hoop from there.

To shoot, you pulled back gently on the appropriate metal lever on your side of the game, then let go. If you didn't pull back far enough, the ball would fall pathetically short of the basket, quickly prompting derisive comments regarding your manhood from your gracious and sensitive opponent. On the other hand, if you pulled the lever back too far, you could launch the ping-pong ball halfway to Mars. When you scored, you turned the cardboard wheel atop your basket to mark another two points for your team. Even if you swished a full-court shot, it was only two points back then rather than three.

Assuming the metal launcher beneath the ball was angled properly, you could score rather consistently from any distance if your muscle memory was good enough. But if your launcher was off track, you'd never come close to the basket. I remember spending many hours on Saturday afternoons in the winter playing a slew of games with my brothers.

Without question, the best indoor hockey game of the 1960s was the one mentioned in the "First Inning" of this memoir. This was the game in which you could direct your players to skate forward or backward by pushing or pulling the long control sticks at your end of the game, and where you could twist the knobs to make them swing their sticks. The goalies only moved from side to side in early versions of the game, but they were wider than other players and would stop pretty much every puck they could touch.

The key to success in this game was dexterity because you could only handle two of the six knobs at one time. Guys who always kept one hand on their goaltenders no matter where the puck was usually couldn't generate much offense. But if you only focused on your center and wings – neglecting your defensemen and netminder – your opponent might steal the puck and fire in a shot from long range before you had time to say "Rogatien Vachon."

* * *

80

Not all the fun we had as children in the 1950s and '60s involved playing sports games, of course. Some of my most vivid memories flood back when I recall games of Kick the Can played after dinner during warm summer evenings. Good hiding places near the can were few and far between, but the darker it got, the easier it was to hide and sneak up on the kid patrolling the region near the can. Once back inside the house, there were plenty of board games to occupy our time before the "lights out" edict, including checkers, Parcheesi, Clue, Monopoly, Rook, Topper and eventually chess.

And while we would take our APBA baseball board game to Cape May, New Jersey every summer, we soon learned that dice don't roll very well on sand. Fortunately, there was a great sport to enjoy right there on the beach. If you're not from the East Coast – and maybe even if you are – there's a good chance you've never heard of this game. It's called Quoits, and the closest activity to it that you're probably familiar with is Horseshoes.

Quoits is an extremely low maintenance sport. All you need are two long, narrow, round steel or wooden pegs to drive into the sand approximately 12 steps apart, and four round, hard-rubber quoits with open middles. Like Horseshoes, the object is to toss your quoits as close to the pole as possible. Standing side-by-side, the two players alternately throw their quoits toward the pin.

After all four are thrown, if one of your quoits ends up closer to the pin than either of your opponent's quoits, you get one point. If both of your quoits are closer than either of your opponent's, you get two points. We always counted leaners as three points and ringers as five. After you've walked toward and picked up the quoits you've thrown, you then toss them toward the other pole. And so on and so forth until one player reaches 21 points to win.

It's considerably more difficult to land a ringer in Quoits than it is in Horseshoes because your quoit first has to clear the top of the peg and then land directly on it. In Horseshoes, you can get a ringer by sliding your horseshoe – open-end first – onto the peg. It's rare to have more than two or three ringers in a game of Quoits.

For a beginner, making quoits land flat is almost as difficult as it is for an experienced player to throw a ringer. It's one of those hand-eye coordination things that you can execute properly nearly every time you toss it once you're used to it. But when you're learning to throw it, the quoit frequently lands on its side and usually rolls away from the pole and downhill toward the surf.

There are a number of strategies you can employ when throwing a quoit, all of which are dependent upon a variety of factors including wind direction and speed, where other quoits are positioned near the peg, the score of the game, and whether the sand on which you're playing is fluffy and dry, packed down and moist, or somewhere in between.

The person who gains one or more points on the previous set of tosses throws the first of the next series of quoits, and the usual tactic is to try to slide a quoit in front of and as close to the pole as possible in order to block that coveted path from one's opponent. If you're unable to accomplish that goal, your opponent will usually attempt to do the same thing with his first of two tosses. You may want to go for a ringer if it looks like your foe is in position to score one or two points and you have the last throw. If you succeed, you'll get five points and your opponent will get shut out.

When I was a kid, we'd go to the beach every day of summer vacation except Sundays, and my grandparents would join us once or twice during our two-week visit. They were both pretty good Quoits players. Granddad enjoyed going for the long ball, so he'd often try to toss ringers, while Mette was more of a singles hitter, very adeptly sliding her quoits near the pole. She would almost always beat Granddad (you live by the homer, you die by the homer), but she frequently received a tougher battle from older brother Bill, younger brother Dave and me. Being very diplomatic, my dad would usually find a way to let Mette defeat him.

We must have played more than 1,000 Quoits games through the years, but a particular contest that stands out in my mind was one in which older brother Bill and I were competing for the annual family championship. It was a best-of-three series and we split the first two games. The third game was very close throughout, but he finally inched ahead by a few points, holding a 19-16 advantage.

Now, both of his quoits were closer to the pin than the one I had tossed and he was anticipating a 21-16 victory and bragging rights for an entire year. My only chance to prevent Bill from winning was to land a clutch ringer with what would probably be my final quoit toss of the summer.

Bill was about 16 years old at the time, and there were plenty of things that were a lot more important to him than Quoits, including girls and cars and girls and running track and girls and the Beach Boys and, oh yes, girls. But not at that moment. Right then, the only thing in his universe that mattered was this Quoits game, and the only thing that concerned him was defeating the skinny, lucky, 10-year-old brother who had been an irritating thorn in his side virtually since the day he was born.

He had worked hard to get to this point, knocking off a cousin in the quarterfinals and edging Dad in the semifinals. And here Bill had put himself into position to claim the summer championship and gloat about it at the dinner table that night, not to mention during the entire 900-mile drive home the following day.

Before I tossed my last quoit, Bill glared at me with a "Don't you dare!" expression on his face. He wasn't trying to intimidate me. It was more like, *You've already used up every lucky break in several lifetimes, so don't even think about cashing in on another one right now.* I was clearly an inferior athlete to Bill at that age, but somehow I had managed to win far more than my share of games against him through the years, often on a fortuitous last at bat, a buzzer-beating shot or a miraculous final quoit throw.

I took a deep breath and aimed carefully, visualizing the perfect quoit toss in my mind. I then stepped forward and released a textbook throw that cut through a slight breeze coming off the ocean and landed dead center on the pole for a ringer, a 21-19 triumph and the family championship. Shouts from my father and Dave pierced the silence and I leaped in the air in celebration.

Remaining perfectly silent, Bill stared at me in disbelief, now undoubtedly wanting to wring my neck or much worse. He knew that kind of behavior would be considered poor sportsmanship, however, so instead he tried to drown himself.

He spun around and raced directly toward the ocean, running as far as he could into the water until a couple of waves battered him down. Then he just stood there in the chest-high surf and gazed out over the horizon for a while, probably wondering what he had done to be so cursed.

Quoits was a lot of fun, but summer vacation didn't last forever. Once back home, baseball was nearly always the game of choice for the boys in our family. No matter how dark or cold it was outside, once you started rolling the dice or flicking the spinner, it was easy to imagine the sun shining brightly, the breeze drifting toward the outfield wall and the pennants waving gently against a deep blue sky. And if you tried hard enough, you could hear the hotdog vendors shouting, the third base coach clapping and the announcers chirping.

Back in those days, when you looked at an APBA baseball card with Willie Mays' name printed in bold letters, you didn't see rows of black and red numbers. You saw a charismatic young man racing out from under his cap to make an over-the-shoulder catch. When you held Frank Robinson's card in your hand, you witnessed a tall, muscular athlete crowding the plate and daring the pitcher to throw at him.

84

When you placed Bob Gibson's card on the table, you observed a no-nonsense, rocking horse-style hurler firing strike after strike. And when you pulled Luis Aparicio's card out of its pack, you beheld an agile shortstop gliding effortlessly toward second base to turn a sure single into a double play.

There's nothing like the real thing in the great outdoors. But back in the Sixties when it was cold or dark outside, it sure was fun spending countless hours playing the indoor games that fed our sports addictions and allowed our imaginations to run wild.

Eighth Inning

Reflecting the Light

The key is lining up the perfect angle. You can employ the biggest weapon in your arsenal and possess the steadiest of hands, but without that precise angle, your efforts will be in vain. The weapon of choice for most of us 11- and 12-year-olds sitting in pews at the Wheaton Bible Church in Wheaton, Illinois on Sunday mornings in the mid-1960s was the metal tie clasp. This accessory was commonly worn by men, as well as by many boys who would rather have been dressed like Little Bo Peep than in itchy, heavy, wool-based suits and clip-on ties.

Back then, lots of us with Protestant parents were required to attend both church and Sunday school on Sunday mornings, and because the 90-minute church service seemed to last about six hours on a good day, we put considerable effort into inventing ways to entertain ourselves and make the time pass more quickly.

One of those activities involved attempting to irritate people sitting in the row in front of us by slowly turning our gleaming silver or gold tie clasps in order to redirect rays of light from the bright fixtures hanging above us into their eyes. The true purpose of a tie clasp is to fasten a tie to your shirt, which is essential because… uh, well, I guess it isn't too important because few people wear them anymore except perhaps high school chemistry teachers. But back then, the tie clasp was a significant part of our Sunday morning wardrobe and if I remember why, I'll mention it later.

When engaging in the highly competitive Tie Clasp Game, the more elderly the person you were able to disturb, the bigger of a stud you were in the eyes of the sophomoric clowns in your pew. This was especially true if you could get one of the ancient folks to rub his eye with a finger or dab it with a handkerchief. Sometimes when we'd relentlessly hone in on a senior citizen's eyeball with this glare, she would actually swat at the air in front of her face as if trying to chase away a pesky gnat. This sent us into hysterics.

The best part of this game, in addition to the obvious thrill a kid that age could experience by annoying older people, was you could do it so subtly that even a suspicious usher would have a difficult time catching you in the act. And the people whose eyes were bothered usually had no clue regarding from whence the ray of light was emanating.

This wasn't the kind of "I saw the light" experience the Social Security-collecting crew was hoping for when they entered the church sanctuary. All they knew was that something bright was crossing back and forth over their eyes and impeding their ability to focus on the sermon.

Paying attention to the message from the pulpit was exactly what we were trying to avoid, and the Tie Clasp Game usually occupied us for a good 15-20 minutes every Sunday morning. This was hardly an insignificant chunk of time when it came to surviving church services clearly designed for adults.

Another time-killer in church was the Dots and Boxes Game. Someone would use as much space on a piece of paper as possible to draw a grid of dots. The two players would then take turns marking a single horizontal or vertical line between two dots until one person was able to complete a square and put his initial inside it. Each time you completed a square, you'd get another turn.

Yet another activity that provided solid entertainment for us was the Hymn Title Game. We'd leaf through the red, hardcover, 350-page hymnal, silently reading the song titles and then adding the phrase, "in the bathtub" at the end of each one.

When you found a good one, you didn't have to spoil the quiet and somber atmosphere in the room by saying a single word. You'd merely nudge the kid next to you and nod your head toward the hymn title. Your friend would know exactly what you were doing and would get just as good of a chuckle out of "There Shall Be Showers of Blessing (in the Bathtub)" as you would. Because you could easily leaf through the entire hymnal during one sermon, this was a game that was played only once every couple of months, but it certainly served its purpose.

Hymnals were also great for making "movies." We'd draw small cartoons in pencil near the ends of the pages, with each succeeding page representing the next "frame" in the film. When you finished – and a good cartoon could easily kill 30 minutes of a sermon – you'd zip through the pages, using your thumb to control the speed.

You and the viewer next to you would enjoy something as entertaining as a large fish chasing and swallowing a small fish, or two cars playing chicken and plowing into each other. Kids who were particularly adept at drawing these cartoons were able to establish a very effective illusion of movement. For all I know, some of them may work for Pixar now.

On Sunday nights, it was far more difficult for me to pass the time in an amusing fashion because I had to sit in the same pew as my parents for the evening service. Most of the kids I hung out with at morning church services and Sunday school weren't required to attend the evening service, and I envied them. Again, this was a gathering totally geared toward adults, yet kids who were unfortunate enough to be in attendance were expected to listen attentively for the entire hour and a half.

I wasn't about to do that. So to make this session more tolerable, I'd add up the number of verses in various books of the Bible, chapter by chapter, and compare the totals to other books in the Bible. My parents didn't seem to mind that I was writing feverishly throughout the sermon because, A) I had my Bible open, and B) I wasn't talking.

From the earliest time I can remember until 18 years of age, a typical week for me in terms of church activities went something like this: Sunday morning was church and then Sunday school, and late Sunday afternoon was youth group, followed by the Sunday evening service. I gotta tell you… I really hated Sundays. Monday night was a youth ministry called Awana, which was pretty cool; Tuesday night was choir practice and Wednesday night was prayer meeting.

On Thursdays, Fridays and Saturdays, there was always at least one evening taken up with something related to church. Summers involved special events such as church camps and Vacation Bible School. As a teenager, I once asked my parents why we didn't arrange to have our mail delivered to the church. They were not amused, but I'm sure they caught my drift.

There was pretty much no way to avoid strict adherence to this schedule through the age of 15 or 16, but once some of my friends who shared my budding rebellious attitude had driver's licenses, we found ways to disappear during the morning church service when our absence would not necessarily be noted. Then we'd show up again when it was time for Sunday school.

Our church was big enough to pull this off, and on the occasions when I'd be questioned by a parent regarding whether I had attended the morning church service, I'd always say I had sat in the balcony. I figured that was safe because none of my parents' friends sat up there. That was a section generally reserved for the "backsliders."

Then I'd casually open my Bible and pull out the church bulletin I had arranged to pick up before the service. And if the interrogation ever became more intense, I'd spout off a few things that had occurred during the service, this knowledge coming courtesy of a friend who had actually been there.

On most of the occasions that we bolted the church parking lot on Sunday mornings, we headed over to Wheaton Bowl a few miles away. One of our friends worked there, so we'd bowl a couple of games for a discounted price before returning to the church. Management didn't seem to mind. Sunday morning at 9 a.m. was not a particularly busy time for the alley, and I think they were glad to have anybody in there, even if we weren't full-fare paying customers.

One time I almost blew it after skipping out on a church service in the late 1960s. On the way to the bowling alley, we learned during a radio broadcast that a prominent Illinois politician had passed away. At the dinner table later that day, I foolishly wondered aloud, to no one in particular, whether anyone had heard that particular piece of news.

My entire family stopped eating and a hush fell over the room. I knew something was up, but had no idea what. My mother then broke the silence by saying, "Yes, Tim, they announced it in church this morning. Were you there to hear it?"

I'm not normally all that quick on my feet and I'm a terrible liar. But in this instance, I managed to pause reflectively and respond, "Yeah, of course I was there. I was sitting in the balcony. I did leave at one point to go to the restroom, but I wasn't gone that long."

One of my helpful older siblings, who assumed I had ditched church, then inquired with a grin, "I wonder why none of your friends mentioned it to you when you came back from the bathroom."

"Knowing them, they probably weren't paying attention," I responded in a reproving tone, feigning disgust over my friends' lack of interest in the church service. "I overheard some adults talking about it in the lobby after church. Looks like I may have to find another group of guys to sit with."

My parents could not possibly have believed this Eddie Haskell-like response, but I think they decided against pursuing the matter any farther because they were just so darn anxious to trust me. Mom and Dad, who had become committed Christians shortly before I was born, must have figured that the more exposure their kids had to church, the more positively we would be influenced.

The theory was certainly well tested, but the results were not good. By the time I was a freshman at Northern Illinois University, I had about as much interest in church as I did in quilting. (No offense to you wonderful quilters out there.) Deep down in my heart, I held the same basic beliefs about God and Christianity my parents did, but I felt as if I had been released from prison when I moved out of my parents' house. The freedom I felt to *not* sit through what I considered incredibly old-fashioned, boring church services intended for older adults was overwhelmingly refreshing to me.

The straight and narrow was very foreign territory to me for a number of years during and following college, and even after I settled down somewhat as a young adult, I just couldn't bring myself to attend church regularly. It seemed like every time I tried out a new church, it reminded me of unpleasant childhood experiences.

Although I didn't vocalize it at the time, I wondered who had established a law that church had to be somber and monotonous. If virtually everything about a church service in the early 1980s was as dull and predictable to a 30-year-old guy as it had been in the early 1960s to a 10-year-old boy, why in the world would anyone willingly go, other than out of guilt? And if I, who still considered himself a Christian, had little interest in attending services, how did church leaders expect to attract people who made no profession of faith, even if they might have been "spiritual seekers?"

Then one day while I was living in Elmhurst, Illinois, a neighbor invited me to a megachurch in the northwest Chicago suburbs called Willow Creek Community Church. I politely told him thanks but no thanks, explaining that I'd attended more church services during the first 18 years of my life than he could in several lifetimes and that the whole issue of church was very depressing for me, even at churches where I agreed with their basic tenants.

But he insisted that this place was different. Instead of a choir, the church featured a band with guitars and drums. Rather than hymns, they sang contemporary, upbeat choruses. Instead of pews, people sat in theater seats. And rather than fire-and-brimstone sermons, they offered relevant, issues-oriented messages. Today there are thousands of churches that fit this mold, but back then I knew of none.

I finally agreed to go in 1983 and when we approached the main entrance, I thought for sure there had been a big accident. Cops with their car lights flashing were directing traffic and nearly every vehicle in a long line of cars and vans was turning toward a huge "campus" off Algonquin Road.

My neighbor explained that it was like this every week, and that it was a good thing we were headed to the 9 a.m. service because it would be even more crowded at 11 a.m. When he told me that approximately 15,000 people attended services at this church every weekend, I was flabbergasted.

Everything he had said about the church was true, but the thing that stood out in my mind for weeks following that service is what was said from the pulpit just before the offering was collected. I had been wondering what kind of hard-sell tactic they were going to utilize to persuade people to put money in the baskets because I had heard them all through the years.

There had to be some way they were paying for the large, modern buildings on their campus, and I figured it might involve pressuring people to give a tithe and an offering, and maybe even sell a body part. But instead, the remarks from the platform went something like this:

"The ushers are going to come forward now and take the

offering. This is a time when members and regular attendees have an opportunity to give back something to God in thanks for all He's done for us. If you're visiting with us, please let the plate pass you by. Keep your money in your wallet. We're just glad you came here today and we want to make you feel at home as our guests."

What?!? No pleas for cash? No guilt trips? No thermometer on the wall telling the congregation how far they're falling short in their responsibility to fund the current project and maybe the pastor's next vacation? What kind of a church is this? It impressed me so much that I actually put some money in the plate.

I didn't sign up for membership that day, but over the next year I began attending more and more often. And after moving closer to the church following the landing of a new job, I became a regular who got involved in a small group Bible study and as a volunteer writer for the church magazine and a sorter in the church's food pantry.

I still wasn't where I felt I needed to be spiritually, but I was finally making some progress after having been dormant for about 15 years. I was also feeling a very gentle but perceptible tug on my heart, which was softening little by little. I had done everything possible for so many years to harden my heart against religion – at least as it manifested itself within the walls of a church building – but I believe God was applying the tenderizer exactly where it was required.

So, what is church like for me now, 30-plus years later? Do I still dread going? Do I attend out of guilt? Do I still play the Tie Clasp Game? Actually, church has become one of the highlights of my week, and that's not just because I have a really boring social life.

And now, instead of redirecting rays of light from a tie clasp into the eyes of annoyed church patrons, I want my life to reflect the light I've received from God. I have plenty more to say on this subject, but this book is primarily a memoir about my formative years and how they were influenced by baseball, so I'm not going to turn it into a spiritual journey story.

My email address is listed at the end. If you're interested in where that journey has taken me, I'd be happy to share that with you... and listen to your story as well.

Ninth Inning

Curses! Foiled Again

Prior to the 2016 season, the Chicago Cubs last won a World Series in 1908. Please read that sentence again. Then read it 106 more times. Done yet? That's how many years had passed since this franchise won a championship. One hundred and eight years! If you think about it, it's really one of the most remarkable things in the world, right up there with the mystery of Stonehenge and the aerodynamic phenomenon of a bee's flight. To give it some perspective, let's take a look at a few of the events that occurred between the Cubs' two most recent Fall Classic titles.

Established in 1966 – 90 years after the Cubs became a charter member of the National League – the Bulls won six NBA titles for the city of Chicago.

The Minnesota Twins won two World Series while playing in an oversized pinball machine known as the Hubert H. Humphrey Metrodome.

The Miami Marlins – the Miami Marlins, for Pete's sake – also won the World Series twice. This is a franchise that didn't even come into existence until 1993.

Commercial radio and television were launched, which meant more Cubs fans were able to hear and see their team lose more often.

Men walked on the moon. Big deal. Cubs pitchers have walked an astronomical number of batters for years and have certainly given up their share of moon shots.

The New York Mets, who entered the National League in 1962

with a modern era record-120 losses and were considered the biggest joke in sports, won it all just seven years later. The Mets also won the World Series in 1986 and played in three others.

The Boston Red Sox, who prior to their 2004 World Series championship had struggled almost as much as the Cubs had through the decades, also captured the Fall Classic in 2007 and 2013. Their previous World Series title came in 1918 against – you guessed it – the Cubs.

Adam and Eve shared an apple. No, wait; that was the year before.

* * *

When the Cubs took a commanding three games-to-one lead over the then-Florida Marlins in the 2003 National League Championship Series with an 8-3 victory at Miami, a miniscule part of my tiny brain actually had the nerve to think, *This is it. This is the year the Cubs will finally make it to the World Series for the first time in my life.*

A bigger part of my mind promptly told the smaller part to shut up. Why? Because I had seen this movie before.

I was 16 years old when the Cubs followed decades of horrible-to-mediocre play with a run for the National League East title in 1969. Billy Williams was swinging sweetly from the left side of the plate, Ron Santo was clicking his heels on the way to the Cubs clubhouse following wins at Wrigley Field and Fergie Jenkins was standing tall and proud on the mound and mowing down hitters. And at 38 years of age, Ernie Banks was using those still-strong wrists to smack home runs while dreaming about finally playing in a Fall Classic to cap off his phenomenal 17-year career.

Because the team had been so awful for nearly my whole life up to that point, I had never witnessed anything like this. The entire Chicago area was buzzing about the Cubs. Not only were more people pouring into Wrigley Field than ever before, but Cubs fans had a radiant glow about them that was contagious. Instead of everybody moping around and wondering how the team was going to lose its next game, they were holding their heads high in anticipation of who the Cubs' next hero would be.

In this first year of division play, the Cubs held an 8½-game lead over the New York Mets in the third week of August. Eight and a half games! There was no way they could possibly blow it with only about 5½ weeks left in the season. Absolutely no way they could let down a huge metropolitan area by failing to advance to the postseason for the 24th consecutive year.

During that summer between my sophomore and junior years of high school, whether or not we had watched that day's game, the one thing brother Dave and I would never miss following a Cubs win was the 10 p.m. news on WGN-TV. Or more specifically, the sports segment of the newscast.

The Cubs were the top sports story nearly every night, and watching highlights of that day's game and hearing the replays of Jack Brickhouse and Lloyd Pettit frantically calling Cubs home runs was the perfect way to end a day. We always hoped that Brickhouse would be at the microphone when the big blasts came. Pettit was a good baseball announcer – although his forte was hockey – but nobody called a home run like an excited Jack Brickhouse.

Immediately following the crack of the bat on a long ball, our ears were in for a tasty treat as Jack's voice jumped an octave as he bellowed, "That's hit! That's waaaay back there. Back... back... BACK... HEY HEY!!! That a boy, Ernie! Wheeeee!!!" It was pure Heaven. It really didn't get any better than that. When Brickhouse was screeching out a home run call – especially if his voice cracked a couple of times – all was right with the world.

In my mind's ear, I can still hear what I believe is Brickhouse's greatest home run call ever. It was Opening Day 1969 and many Cubs fans had high hopes for the season after seeing steady improvement the past couple of years. The Cubs and Phillies were engaged in a donnybrook at Wrigley Field, with Banks and Philly's Don Money having belted two home runs each. Trailing 6-5, the Cubs were coming to bat in the bottom of the 11th inning. Randy Hundley singled with one out and Willie Smith marched to the plate as a pinch-hitter, taking his place in the left-hander's batter's box.

"That's pretty well hit. It's way back there. Back… back… back… HEY HEY!!! It's a homer!!! Willie Smith just homered!!! THE CUBS WIN THE GAME!!!"

I still get goose bumps listening to that call. There's no way in words alone to do justice to the vocal delights that Brickhouse generated with his incredible enthusiasm. But if you've been a Cubs fan for a long time and enjoyed the late broadcaster's home run calls, I'm guessing you probably "heard" them again while you were reading those last few paragraphs. If you never heard Brickhouse call a homer – or if you just want to be reminded of his unique style – Google a few of them on YouTube.

I can't remember whether it was during the 1969 season, but at some point WGN-TV hired Ernie Banks to handle the sports segment of the news on Sunday nights when the Cubs were in town. Journalism wasn't Ernie's strong suit, but he got through it. One of the things I enjoyed most about Banks' performance behind the news desk was when he would set up a highlight by humbly saying, "and then I came to bat." Then you'd see good old number 14 launching a drive onto Waveland Avenue and hear Brickhouse or Pettit or occasionally Lou Boudreau going nuts.

Speaking of Boudreau, one of his unintentionally entertaining habits while describing an outfield fly involved him saying, "There's a high fly… Clemente over… he's waiting for it to come down… and it does." As if there were any doubt that the ball would eventually return to Earth.

Brickhouse, who also announced White Sox games for a while, would sometimes do the play-by-play for other Chicago sports teams as well, including the Bears and Bulls. He'd always put in a great effort, but it was never the same as when he announced the diamond game. Some of his football verbal mainstays were, "There's the punt… it's a high spiral, traveling north," like you'd care which direction the punt was moving. Or he'd say, "Sayers is brought down at the 28 or 29-yard line… we'll call it the 34." It was always entertaining when Jack would get excited about a big defensive play by the Bears. "And Willard is mobbed by Butkus, Buffone, O'Bradovich, Atkins… and a HOST of Chicago Bears."

During a Bulls game, you could always count on Jack using his favorite basketball phrase at the beginning of the telecast – "Here are the greatest basketball players in the world" – no matter who the Bulls were playing, and getting his words mixed up when the action became fast paced, such as, "There's Guy Rodgers with his patented behind-the-pass-back."

Nobody was more entertaining than Lou Boudreau when he'd periodically fill in on a Blackhawks broadcast. Extremely knowledgeable about baseball, Lou was definitely on thin ice when it came to sticks and pucks. And even when he got the commentary correct, you knew he was always right on the verge of butchering another French name, such as Henri Richard or Yvan Cournoyer. Which is kind of ironic if you think about it, because isn't Boudreau a French name?

Pettit, on the other hand, was a remarkable hockey announcer. His patented, "A shot and a goal!" has been repeated countless times by Hawks fans through the years. He also had a couple of catchphrases for when a puck would sail into the crowd. One of them was, "We lose a puck and gain a faceoff," while the other was, "That baby had some mustard on it. Hope everybody's OK."

And when Pettit would call a hockey fight, it was usually something along the lines of, "Magnuson and Vadnais. Magnuson and Vadnais. Vadnais and Magnuson. A right! Another right! A left!" It was the perfect, understated account if you were watching on television, but when it was a radio broadcast, you had absolutely no idea who was winning the fight. You sure did enjoy listening to it, though.

Nobody took any pleasure in listening to Cubs games after their swan dive began in late August of 1969. Except, that is, for Mets and White Sox fans. Just when it looked like the division title was in the bag, everything that could possibly go wrong did. At the exact same time the Miracle Mets were becoming virtually unbeatable, the Cubs couldn't win a game to save their lives.

And after a black cat walked in front of the Cubs dugout at Shea Stadium during a night game, well, that was pretty much the handwriting on the wall, the straw that broke the camel's back, the end of the world as we know it, and any other cliché you'd like to toss in.

I've heard people say, "The Cubs didn't lose the National League East Division in 1969, the Mets won it." Yes, the Mets played incredible baseball during those last seven weeks, winning 38 of 49. But I'm sorry. You can't go from an 8½-game lead to trailing by eight games without a complete collapse featuring a healthy dose of choking.

As sad as we Cubs fans were after such a promising season, we felt even worse for Ernie Banks. Mr. Cub deserved to play in a World Series more than anybody in the league, and we all feared he'd never get another chance. Unfortunately, we were right.

Ernie's lack of a World Series ring was one of the things we were reminded of when he passed away from a heart attack in 2015, just shy of his 84th birthday. I lost a piece of myself that day, and I know countless other baseball fans did as well. It was all anybody could talk about in the days that followed.

Fast forward 15 years from 1969. Following a number of brutal seasons, the Cubs made some shrewd moves, picking up key players such as pitchers Rick Sutcliffe and Dennis Eckersley, plus outfielders Gary Matthews and Bobby Dernier. The Cubs marched all the way to the National League East title in 1984 and took a seemingly comfortable two games-to-none lead in the best-of-five League Championship Series over the San Diego Padres with a pair of wins at Wrigley Field.

I wasn't able to attend either of those playoff games, but I watched both of them with friends at an establishment in Elmhurst, Illinois. Believe it or not, I actually kept a box score of both games, right there in the bar. There may have been a bigger 31-year-old geek in the world at the time, but I doubt it. I just couldn't resist recording a personal chronicle of what I figured could well be a once-in-a-lifetime experience... the Cubs going to the World Series.

Few Cubs fan were worried when their team dropped Game 3, but after a heartbreaking 7-5 defeat on a Saturday night featuring Steve Garvey's heroics for the Padres, the city of Chicago shook its collective head and wondered aloud how the Cubs would manage to blow the decisive Game 5 and lose out on a golden opportunity to advance to the World Series for the first time since 1945.

I decided to watch Game 5 at home. By myself. I didn't want to be around anybody when the Cubs messed up again. On the other hand, I didn't wish to celebrate solo if they did happen to win. So, I figured that if the Cubs held a lead heading into the eighth inning, I'd make the five-minute drive to the Elmhurst bar at which I'd viewed Games 1, 2 and 4, joining in the celebration there if the Cubs hung on to win.

The Cubs grabbed a 3-0 advantage in the second inning of that fateful fifth game of the NLCS on homers by Leon Durham and Jody

Davis, and I changed into a decent pair of jeans and a shirt in order to look presentable around other people. But then the roof caved in. After pulling to within one run, the Padres tallied four times in the bottom of the seventh, tying the game when a ground ball went through the legs of Durham at first base. Everybody knew it was over at that point, and sure enough San Diego went on to win 6-3 and capture the series with its third consecutive victory. Cubs fans across the country sank into a deep depression.

Before I started sulking, however, there was a little business to attend to in the basement of the house I was renting. Letting loose with years of frustration and fury, I invented new combinations of colorful words and broke virtually everything within reach that I owned, including lamps, pottery and a couple of pictures on the wall. Pretty mature, huh?

Larry, my roommate and a White Sox fan who was at work when my explosion occurred, understood. After arriving home and checking on the carnage in the basement – then seeing me sitting on the couch with a dour look on my face – he offered, "At least your team got in the playoffs this year."

That just wasn't enough for me. I was absolutely infuriated that the team I had faithfully followed and supported for so many years had let me down so cruelly. Many Cubs fans shared my grief and anger, but some of them were a little too quick to say, "Wait 'til next year." I was eventually able to spout that tired phrase, but it took a while. This team deserved to be ripped for blowing it, and I think a lot of Cubs fans were too forgiving too soon.

Five years later, the Cubs garnered another division crown, but the disappointment was not nearly as severe when they were manhandled four games to one by San Francisco in the NLCS. Even the three-game sweep at the hands of the Braves in the first round of the 1998 playoffs was bearable because the Cubs had just squeaked into the postseason with a one-game playoff win over the Giants to capture the

102

Wild Card berth, and nobody expected them to dislodge a strong Atlanta team.

In 2003, the Cubs mirrored their 1984 regular season, adding key players both before and during the campaign to capture the division title. With fleet-footed center fielder Kenny Lofton, slugging third baseman Aramis Ramirez and free-swinging Randall Simon now wearing Cubbie blue – all courtesy of the Pittsburgh Pirates – the Cubs battled Houston and St. Louis throughout the season before gaining the top spot in the Central Division on the final weekend.

Once again the vaunted Braves were the playoff opponents, but this time the Cubs rose to the task at hand. With Kerry Wood winning two games and Moises Alou and Eric Karros providing offensive punch, Chicago earned a hard-fought, three games-to-two Division Series triumph.

I had thought maybe I'd get to share in a division series-clinching celebration while sitting in the grandstands behind third base for Game 4. It had been a long time since I felt an atmosphere so electric at Wrigley Field. Nearly all of us in this packed house were on our feet for at least half the game, screaming at the top of our lungs.

The Cubs led early and then rallied late in this one, but couldn't quite pull it off, losing 6-4. However, it was a very interesting game that featured a little bit of everything. Braves left fielder Chipper Jones hadn't been swinging the bat very well in the series, but he more than made up for it with a pair of two-run homers that seemed to hang in the air forever.

Eric Karros contributed two dingers for the Cubs, but both were solo shots. And that was the key to this one. The Cubs' top three men in the batting order – Lofton, Mark Grudzielanek and Sammy Sosa – were a combined 1-for-13. They just couldn't set the table for the middle of the order.

103

The most bizarre play in this game occurred in the eighth inning. Braves pinch-hitter Robert Fick tried to reach base via a bunt, and when he realized he was going to be out, flung his arm out and struck Karros' left arm, knocking the ball out of his glove. Perhaps Fick was trying to execute the tomahawk chop Braves fans like to do when their team is rallying... and that fans of opposing teams enjoy imitating in a mocking fashion when the Braves are struggling.

Fick was declared out for interference on the play, and when it appeared that Karros might be injured, about 40,000 of us let Fick know exactly what we thought of him in rather loud and unflattering terms. Karros, who recovered to hit his second home run of the game in the bottom half of the inning, was later quoted as saying, "It's an interesting running technique, and that's all I'll say about it."

Down 6-3 heading into the bottom of the ninth, the Cubs pulled to within two runs when Simon and Damian Miller both doubled. Representing the tying run with two outs, Sosa took John Smoltz deep... but not deep enough. Center fielder Andruw Jones hauled in Sosa's fly ball at the warning track to end the game. Wood then came up huge in Game 5 in Atlanta to allow the Cubs to advance to the NLCS against the surprising Florida Marlins.

I also attended the 2003 League Championship Series opener against the Marlins at Wrigley Field and the aura was even more charged this time. The first 10 hits in this wild ballgame went for extra bases, and in fact the two teams established an LCS standard with 17 hits of the extra-base variety.

Things started out great on this freakishly warm (75 degrees) mid-October evening when Chicago raced to a 4-0 lead in the first inning, thanks in part to Alou's two-run homer onto Waveland Avenue. But pitcher Carlos Zambrano, who had given up only nine homers the entire season, looked like he was pitching batting practice in the third inning when he allowed the Marlins to set an NLCS record with three circuit clouts in the same frame.

I didn't think this see-saw game in front of 39,567 screaming lunatics – plus countless thousands camped out on the surrounding streets – could get any more exciting, but Alex Gonzalez proved me wrong by pounding a two-run homer that tied it at 6-6 in the sixth. The Cubs fell behind again, 8-6, and only Sosa's clutch homer with two outs in the bottom of the ninth kept the Cubs' hopes alive.

But Mike Lowell's solo homer in the 11th inning sealed the Cubs' fate, and that loss would come back to haunt them. In fact, if the Cubs hadn't blown that opener, they could have swept the series and no one would have ever heard of Steve Bartman, which I'm certain would have been fine with him.

To their credit, the Cubs rallied to win the next three games and come within one victory of their first World Series appearance in 58 years. In fact, I'm not sure Sosa's Game 2 home run to straightaway center field has landed yet. But it just wasn't meant to be… again. The Game 6 loss featuring the famous foul ball that was deflected away from Moises Alou by the ill-fated fan, and the Game 7 fiasco in which the Cubs blew a 5-3 lead, turned a city on the verge of an eruption into a morgue.

* * *

A myriad of excuses has been offered through the years for the Cubs' inability to win a championship between 1908 and 2015. Too many day games at Wrigley Field and the black cat were popular ones in 1969, while Gatorade spilling on Durham's glove was the scapegoat in 1984. Bartman was castigated for the 2003 flop, but anybody with an ounce of decency and half a brain realizes the ridiculousness of that kind of finger pointing. I've watched that replay at least 25 times and I'd be willing to bet that 99 out of 100 fans would have done exactly the same thing Bartman did. (The 100th person would have actually caught the ball.)

If you examine that play closely, you'll see Bartman and every other fan in his section following the flight of the high foul ball as it slowly drifted back toward them and the playing field. If you've ever been at a baseball game when a foul ball was coming your way, you know that your first instinct is to protect yourself and your second is to try to catch it.

You're looking straight up at the ball, not at the closest fielder. From that vantage point, it's virtually impossible to tell if the ball is drifting or if it's coming straight down. And if the choice appears to be either getting hit with the rock-hard sphere or trying to catch it, you're going to do the latter. As it turned out, the ball hooked back toward the field of play just enough that Alou, standing near the padded wall, probably could have caught it had it not bounced off Bartman's hands.

Alou was understandably upset that he was not given the chance to make a play on the ball, but in retrospect, the anger he immediately directed toward Bartman only served to help make the young man an unwitting target who needed to be escorted from that section of the park before drunken fans pummeled him. What everyone seems to forget is that shortstop Alex Gonzalez could have put the entire matter to rest had he turned a subsequent grounder into a double play instead of botching it for the error that really opened the floodgates. Florida ended up scoring eight runs in that eighth inning of Game 6, then captured the pennant the following night with a Game 7 victory.

Cubs fans who still blame Bartman for ruining the team's chances in 2003 are as confused as many of the Cubs owners who have fielded the ill-equipped and mismanaged players wearing Cubs uniforms for much of the past 10 decades.

The only explanation that seemed to make any sense for the Cubs' lack of a World Series title in more than 100 years prior to 2016 is the Curse of the Goat. For those of you unfamiliar with the story, it seems that in 1945, Billy Goat Tavern owner William Sianis tried to enter Wrigley Field for Game 4 of the World Series against the Detroit Tigers with his goat.

Apparently this act was intended to promote his business. By the way, this is the same tavern that was parodied in *Saturday Night Live* skits featuring John Belushi, Dan Aykroyd and Bill Murray serving up "cheeseburger cheeseburger" and informing customers that they offered "Pepsi no Coke" and "chips no fries."

Sianis, who was allegedly denied admission to the park unless he first agreed to park his animal at the curb, was infuriated. And after all, who wouldn't be ticked off if he were not allowed to take a four-hoofed animal into a professional sporting event? Legend has it the bar owner loudly declared that this outrageous slight would result in a curse being placed on the Cubs – there would never again be a World Series at Wrigley Field.

Anyone who scoffed at such a notion at the time is probably… well, they're probably dead by now. But prior to the 2016 championship, Cubs fans had to be thinking that maybe there was some legitimacy to the curse. How else could it have been explained? The Cubs certainly won their share of National League pennants prior to the Curse in the 1930s – although most of the time they couldn't quite make it happen in the Fall Classic – but since 1945 then there have been very few legitimate threats by the North Siders.

It can definitely be argued that Cubs management did not place its best foot forward for a 20-season span between 1947 and 1966. This was a wasteland of a franchise that failed to finish in the top half of the National League standings even once during those 20 lost seasons. Not once! They did manage to finish last on five occasions, however, including in 1966 when their 59-103 record was even worse than both the two recent N.L. expansion teams' marks.

More recently, under Chicago Tribune Company ownership, the team spent plenty of money, and general manager Jim Hendry often did an exceptional job of picking up the right player at the ideal time. It's clearly not his fault – nor Bartman's – that the Cubs threw away the pennant in 2003 when all they needed was one Wrigley Field win in two chances and their pair of aces – Mark Prior and Kerry Wood – going for them in Games 6 and 7 of the NLCS.

In 2009, the Cubs were purchased by the Ricketts family, who hired Theo Epstein as their president of baseball operations. Epstein was primarily responsible for putting the Boston Red Sox team together that won a World Series in 2004 for the first time in 86 years – not to mention World Series crowns in 2007 and 2013 – so who better to pull off a miracle in Chicago?

The first few years were ugly – as Epstein warned they would be while he stockpiled plenty of young talent – but in 2015 the Cubs produced the third-best record in baseball, defeated Pittsburgh in a one-game Wild Card playoff and then knocked off St. Louis three games to one in a Division Series. That's when the Cubs ran out of steam, being swept by the hated Mets in the League Championship Series.

The Cubs franchise really did appear to be cursed until 2016. Maybe it wasn't the Billy Goat Curse, but something or somebody didn't seem to want this team to win a World Series. Between 1945 and 2015, the best way to ensure that outcome was to keep them from playing in one. Think about how many Cubs fans must have been born and died between the 1908 and 2016 World Series titles. Maybe now in the afterlife they know if the Cubs were cursed, but we sure don't.

When the guy your franchise calls "Mr. Cub" never even came close to a World Series, how sad is that? But that was the case for shortstop-turned-first baseman Ernie Banks. Many longtime Cubs fans would have given just about anything to see Mr. Sunshine play in just one World Series in front of a national audience. Just one.

The repetitive, underhand practice swing, the right elbow held high, the long fingers dancing at the bottom of the bat handle… Ernie was a pure pleasure to watch in the batter's box. His wrists were so quick that he could afford to wait a long time before making up his mind whether to swing at a pitch. And when he did, his bat speed was amazing as he'd light into a fastball and send it rocketing over the left fielder's head and into the sun-drenched bleachers.

I'm afraid those days are long gone. But now that the Cubs have finally put it all together and won the World Series, this championship should be dedicated to good old number 14. There is nobody more deserving.

Extra Innings

2016

When something hasn't happened during the first 50, 60 or 70 years of your life, it's a pretty safe bet that it won't. Not an absolute certainty, mind you, but it's very unlikely.

If you've never married by then, it's doubtful you'll be tying the knot anytime soon. If you haven't had any kids yet, chances are you won't be buying any baby name books. If you've never held a job for more than a year, well, you're probably not going to be offered a long-term contract anywhere.

And if your favorite baseball team hasn't won a World Series in your lifetime, it's very possible that it's just not meant to be. At least that's what I used to think. Fortunately, the Chicago Cubs proved me wrong in 2016 and now I can cross "celebrating a World Series championship" off my bucket list.

Let's take a quick look at the Cubs' 2016 season. I have a feeling I'm going to be reliving this thing over and over again until Opening Day 2017.

The Cubs started the 2016 campaign in fine fashion, defeating the host Los Angeles Angels of Anaheim 9-0 on Opening Day. Jake Arrieta pitched seven innings of two-hit ball, striking out six batters along the way. Centerfielder Dexter Fowler set the tone for his exceptional season with a 3-for-4 performance and three runs scored, while catcher Miguel Montero was 2-for-5 with a two-run homer and three RBI. Chicago went 5-1 on that road trip, outscoring the Angels and Arizona Diamondbacks by a cumulative 42-15 score.

A three-game sweep of Cincinnati at the Friendly Confines

followed, and it was obvious the Cubs were on their way to accomplishing something special. Following their final game of April, they were 17-5 and held a 3½-game lead in the National League Central Division.

Chicago lost twice as many games in May as it did in April, but still put together an 18-10 month, thanks to an eight-game winning streak early in the month and a six-game win streak near the end. The Cubs were now 35-15, 6½ games ahead of the rest of the pack.

June and July were not exactly stellar months for the Northsiders, who barely played .500 ball (28-26). They lost six out of seven games to St. Louis and Miami in late June, then dropped nine of 10 through July 9, beginning with a four-game sweep at the hands of the New York Mets at Citi Field. But they still held a 7½-game division lead entering August.

It was a far different story in August, as the Cubs went 22-6. An 11-game winning streak ended on August 13 versus the Cardinals, but before the month concluded, Chicago put a couple of four-game winning streaks together.

The Cubs clinched their first Central Division title since 2008 when St. Louis lost at San Francisco on September 15, celebrating the following day after a dramatic win over the Milwaukee Brewers at Wrigley Field. Chicago trailed 4-2 heading into the bottom of the ninth inning, but rallied to send it into extra innings on RBI singles by Chris Coghlan and Addison Russell. Montero then won it with a walk-off homer to lead off the bottom of the 10th. It brought the Cubs' record to 94-53 with 15 games to play.

Chicago racked up its 100th win of the season with a 12-2 rout at Pittsburgh on September 26. Kyle Hendricks improved his record to 16-8 and six Cubs players had multiple hit games, including Javier Baez (grand slam), Kris Bryant (39th home run) and Albert Almora (3-for-6).

It marked only the sixth time in franchise history that a Cubs team won 100 regular-season games. The last time it happened was 1935 when Chicago was led by 20-game winners Bill Lee and Lon Warneke; catcher and league MVP Gabby Hartnett (.344 batting average, 91 RBI); and second baseman Billy Herman (.341) and outfielder Chuck Klein (team-high 21 homers).

Even with little to play for down the stretch, the Cubs won nine of their last 13 regular-season games (tying one in a rain-shortened game) to finish 103-58, 17½ games ahead of the St. Louis Cardinals.

For the 2016 regular season, the Cubs were 57-24 at Wrigley Field and 46-34 on the road. Chicago posted a 42-13 record in games decided by five or more runs, but only a 22-23 mark in one-run affairs. In addition to making life miserable for most N.L. teams, the Cubs feasted on American League foes by winning 15 of 20 contests.

Chicago finished 15-4 versus Cincinnati, 14-4-1 against Pittsburgh, 11-8 versus Milwaukee, 5-1 against Philadelphia, and 5-2 versus Washington and Arizona. Of the 20 teams the Cubs faced, the only ones to get the better of them in 2016 were the New York Mets (5-2) and Colorado (4-2). They split their season series with Atlanta (3-3).

The Cubs outscored their opponents 808-556 during the 2016 regular season and a look at their individual player stats shows why.

Third baseman Kris Bryant hit .292 with 39 home runs, 102 RBI and a team-high 121 runs scored, while first baseman Anthony Rizzo also batted .292 with 32 homers and 109 RBI. Leadoff man Dexter Fowler posted team highs in on-base percentage (.393) and stolen bases (13), and second baseman/outfielder Ben Zobrist hit .272 with 18 home runs and 76 RBI. Shortstop Addison Russell contributed 21 home runs and 95 RBI, while infielder Javier Baez batted .273 with 14 homers and 59 RBI.

The Cubs' top five starters were magnificent. Left-hander Jon

Lester posted a 19-5 record with a 2.44 earned run average and a team-high 197 strikeouts, while righty Kyle Hendricks went 16-8 with a league-best 2.13 ERA. Jake Arrieta, who entered the season as the team's ace, won 18 of his 26 decisions with a 3.10 ERA and 190 strikeouts. Jason Hammel and John Lackey combined for 26 wins and 324 strikeouts. Relievers Hector Rondon and Aroldis Chapman totaled 34 saves between them, with Chapman crafting a 1.01 ERA in 28 appearances for the Cubs after coming over from the New York Yankees.

* * *

Before examining the Cubs' exciting postseason run, I think it's a good idea to remember how long it had been since they won a World Series. In 1908 – a leap year, like 2016 – William Howard Taft defeated William Jennings Bryan in the presidential election and Henry Ford produced his first Model T automobile.

Among those who passed away that year were 22nd and 24th President Grover Cleveland and outlaws Butch Cassidy and the Sundance Kid. Just beginning their lives in 1908 were actors Bette Davis, Jimmy Stewart and Fred MacMurray; 36th President Lyndon Johnson and businessman and 41st Vice President Nelson Rockefeller; comedian Milton Berle; and gangster Baby Face Nelson.

The Cubs' 2016 postseason began on Friday, October 7 at the Friendly Confines. A matchup of Jon Lester and San Francisco's Johnny Cueto foretold a pitcher's duel, and that's exactly what a raucous crowd of 42,148 witnessed. If those Cubs fans had known their team would manage only one run on three hits for the night, they would not have expected a victory.

Chicago did not produce its first hit – a double to left field by Kris Bryant – until the fourth inning. Following a harmless fifth-inning single by Javy Baez, Cueto seemed to get even stronger, retiring the next eight batters he faced and striking out five of them. Unfortunately for Cueto and the Giants, Lester was only slightly less dominant.

The left-hander gave up leadoff singles in each of the first three innings, then allowed a single and a double in the fourth. But he was able to strand every base runner, thanks in part to catcher David Ross throwing out one would-be base stealer at second and picking another runner off first. Lester then retired the Giants in order in the fifth through the eighth innings.

It was still scoreless when Baez drilled a Cueto pitch that might have hit a building on Waveland Avenue had a stiff breeze not knocked it down. Left fielder Angel Pagan set himself up to make the catch at the wall, but it fell into the basket for a home run and what turned out to be the only run of the game.

Lester gave way in the top of the ninth inning to fire-balling lefty Aroldis Chapman, who allowed a two-out double to Buster Posey before sending the crowd into a frenzy by inducing a game-ending groundout by Hunter Pence. The Giants finished with twice as many hits as the Cubs, but couldn't dent home plate and fell behind one game to none in the series following the 1-0 loss.

In Game Two the following evening, all seven runs were scored in the first four innings. The Cubs grabbed a 1-0 lead in the bottom of the first when Dexter Fowler doubled off the right-centerfield wall and raced home on a two-out single by Ben Zobrist.

Chicago came back with three more runs in the second frame off Giants starter and former Cubs pitcher Jeff Samardzija. The Cubs loaded the bases on a double by Jason Heyward, a walk to Baez and a single by Willson Contreras. The Giants were looking for a bunt with pitcher Kyle Hendricks at the plate, but he surprised everyone by stroking a two-run single into centerfield. One out later, Bryant singled home Contreras, and the Cubs led 4-0.

San Francisco cut its deficit in half in the third inning on back-

114

to-back doubles by Joe Panik and Gregor Blanco, and a sacrifice fly by Brandon Belt. But the Giants accomplished something with the potential for much more damage with two outs in the fourth when Pagan smashed a line drive off the right forearm of Hendricks, who was forced to leave the game with a contusion.

But never fear, Travis Wood was there. The left-handed reliever came in and retired Conor Gillaspie, who had won the Wild Card game over the New York Mets with a three-run homer three nights earlier, to maintain Chicago's 4-2 lead. Wood wasn't finished... not by a long shot. He belted a solo home run into the left field bleachers in the bottom of the fourth, then shut down the visitors in the fifth.

The Cubs bullpen continued to shine the rest of the night. Carl Edwards Jr., Mike Montgomery, Hector Rondon and Chapman held San Francisco scoreless over the final four innings, allowing two singles and no walks. The 5-2 triumph gave Chicago a 2-0 lead in the series heading to the West Coast.

In Game Three, the Cubs came tantalizingly close to sweeping the series, but couldn't get the job done. Billed as a matchup between two stellar moundsmen – 2015 Cy Young Award winner Jake Arrieta and 2014 World Series MVP Madison Bumgarner – this wild affair eventually turned the spotlight on a variety of other players.

Before it did, however, Arrieta silenced a screaming throng by lashing a three-run homer into the left field seats off Bumgarner for a 3-0 lead in the top of the second inning. But the Cubs left at least one runner on base in five of the next six innings while being blanked by several Giants pitchers. San Francisco, meanwhile, chipped away at the lead before scoring three times in the eighth for a 5-3 advantage.

With Giants closer Sergio Romo on the hill in the ninth, Dexter Fowler walked and Kris Bryant lofted a game-tying homer that bounced on top of the left field wall. Mike Montgomery did everything he could to keep the Giants in check over the next few innings, but back-to-back doubles in the 13th frame won it 6-5 for the home team.

When Cubs fans look back on this magical season in years to come, they will remember Game Four of this Division Series. The Giants, victors in three of the past six World Series and winners of 10 consecutive elimination games, led in this one 5-2 entering the ninth inning. David Ross had become the oldest Cubs player in history to produce a postseason home run when he tied the game at 1-1 back in the third inning with a solo shot, yet the Cubs had not managed a hit since Anthony Rizzo's fourth-inning single.

But after Bryant singled and Rizzo walked, Ben Zobrist doubled to right field to make it 5-3 with no outs. With the fourth Giants pitcher of the inning entering the game, pinch-hitter Willson Contreras produced a two-run single to center to plate both base runners and tie the game. Jason Heyward then bunted into a force out, took second on an error and scored the lead run on Javy Baez's clutch single up the middle.

Chapman came on to pitch, and unlike the previous evening when he faltered, struck out all three batters he faced to give the Cubs one of the greatest comeback victories in postseason history, 6-5.

For the series, Baez and Bryant both hit .375, but most of the other Cubs regulars struggled at the plate. On the hill, Jon Lester posted a 0.00 ERA over eight innings, while Chapman earned three saves, Mike Montgomery crafted a 1.69 ERA, and Hector Rondon and Travis Wood picked up wins.

While the Cubs finished their division series on Tuesday night, October 11, the Los Angeles Dodgers did not wrap up their series until Thursday night the 13th. Those two extra days of rest figured to help the Cubs, who began the National League Championship Series at home for the second straight season.

If you had tickets for one of the first two NLCS games at Wrigley Field, I sure hope it was the first one. Game 1 was one of the most thrilling contests in Cubs history, while Game 2 was a frustrating mess. Let's get the negative stuff out of the way first.

After taking a 1-0 series lead, Chicago faced left-hander Clayton Kershaw, whose credentials are impeccable. The three-time Cy Young Award winner, six-time All-Star, four-time National League ERA leader, three-time league strikeout king, two-time N.L. wins leader and 2014 N.L. Most Valuable Player had recently won one game and saved another in the five-game Division Series triumph over the Washington Nationals.

The Cubs' only hope against this other-worldly left-hander was that Kershaw would be too exhausted to be effective in Game 2. He wasn't. Dodgers first baseman Adrian Gonzalez lofted an opposite field home run into the left field bleachers in the second inning, and it was all Kershaw needed to earn the 1-0 win. He allowed only two singles and one walk in seven innings, striking out six. For the Cubs, Kyle Hendricks had control issues, walking four, but allowed only three hits in 5.1 innings.

The NLCS opener had been much more fun to watch. The Cubs took a 1-0 lead in the first inning on a single by Dexter Fowler and an RBI double by Kris Bryant, then added two more runs in the second on Jason Heyward's triple and Javy Baez's RBI double and steal of home.

The Dodgers nibbled away with one run in the fifth and two more in the eighth to tie the game at 3-3. That's when things got interesting. In the bottom of the eighth, Ben Zobrist doubled to put the potential lead run in scoring position, followed by Addison Russell's groundout and an intentional walk to Heyward. Following a fly out by Baez, pinch-hitter Chris Coughlin was issued an intentional pass to fill the bases.

With the crowd of 42,376 already on its feet, pinch-hitter

117

Miguel Montero slammed a Joe Blanton pitch deep into the right field bleachers for a grand slam and a 7-3 Cubs lead, sparking a celebration that literally shook the building, according to television announcers. Fowler followed with a solo shot to right off Blanton for an 8-3 advantage.

The Dodgers got one of those runs back in the top of the ninth, but fell 8-4. Despite not having his best stuff, Jon Lester gave up only one run in six innings. Aroldis Chapman, one of six Cubs relievers, was credited with the win. Fowler, Bryant and Baez had two hits apiece for the winners.

In Game 3 at Dodger Stadium, the Cubs hitting woes continued as they stretched their scoreless streak from nine to 18 innings. Southpaw Rich Hill picked up where Kershaw left off, shutting out Chicago on two hits and striking out a half-dozen in six innings. L.A. catcher Yasmani Grandal took Jake Arrieta deep with a two-run homer in the fourth inning, and third baseman Justin Turner added a solo shot in the sixth on the way to a 6-0 Dodgers victory.

Desperately needing a win in Game 4, the Cubs responded in a big way. Their 10-2 triumph featured a four-run fourth inning and a five-run sixth as the bats finally came alive off starter Julio Urias and his relievers. Picking up the win in relief was Mike Montgomery, who took over when starter John Lackey walked the first two batters in the fifth inning.

Anthony Rizzo and Addison Russell broke out of their slumps, both going 3-for-5 with a home run. Dexter Fowler and Ben Zobrist added two hits apiece. In the fourth frame, the Cubs ended their 21-inning scoring doldrums with consecutive singles by Zobrist, Javy Baez and Willson Contreras, an RBI groundout by Jason Heyward, and Russell's two-run dinger. Rizzo connected for a solo homer in the fifth, then produced a two-run single in the sixth.

In what many were calling a "must-win" for the Cubs – due to

118

Kershaw being scheduled to pitch Game 6 – Chicago rose to the occasion with an 8-4 Game 5 victory at Los Angeles. Lester was masterful once again, limiting the Dodgers to one run on five hits while striking out six in seven innings. Relievers Pedro Strop and Chapman struggled in the eighth and ninth innings, but the Cubs had enough of a cushion to hang on for the win.

The Cubbies led 3-1 entering the eighth inning after repeatedly failing to bring home runners in scoring position all game long. But they had their way with relievers Pedro Baez and Ross Stripling during a five-run eighth. After Russell reached on an error and Contreras singled him to second, pinch-hitter Albert Almora sacrificed them to second and third.

Fowler and Bryant came through with RBI infield singles, and one out later, Zobrist walked to fill the bases. Javy Baez then doubled down the right field line to drive in all three base runners. The Cubs flew back to Chicago with a three-games-to-two lead in the NLCS, just one win away from their first World Series appearance in 71 years. Would the curse rear its ugly head, or were the Cubs destined to break that curse?

In Game 6 at Wrigley Field on October 22, 2016, the electricity in the air could have powered the entire lighting system. Cubs fans were pumped up to see history made. Only one thing seemed to have a chance of derailing the franchise's first appearance in the Fall Classic since 1945. And that was a pitcher named Clayton Kershaw. The bottom line was this: would Chicago's Kyle Hendricks be able to rise to the occasion and outpitch Kershaw. The early returns said "yes."

L.A.'s Andrew Toles lined the first pitch of the game into right field for a single, but Corey Seager grounded the second pitch to second baseman Javy Baez, who charged in, scooped it up, tagged Toles and fired to first for a double play. Justin Turner then flew out to right field for the Dodgers' first goose egg of the game.

119

In the bottom of the first, Dexter Fowler stroked an opposite field, ground rule double and Kris Bryant followed with an RBI single, again to right field. Anthony Rizzo then hit what appeared to be a routine line drive to left field. But Toles took his eyes off the ball for an instant and it clanked off his glove for a two-base error. Ben Zobrist lofted a sacrifice fly to centerfield, and the Cubs led 2-0 after one inning.

The Cubs added to their lead in the second inning when Addison Russell doubled down the left field line and scored on a clutch, two-run single by Fowler. Following a scoreless third frame, Chicago made it 4-0 when catcher Willson Contreras ripped a home run into the left field bleachers, making him the third Cubs backstop to homer in the series. Then with two outs in the bottom of the fifth and Kershaw seeming to have settled down, Anthony Rizzo took him deep to right-center for a 5-0 Cubs advantage.

Meanwhile, Hendricks was showing the world why he was a 2016 Cy Young Award candidate. By the time he left the game with one out in the top of the eighth, the steady right-hander had allowed no runs on two hits and no walks, striking out six and facing only two batters over the minimum.

Dodgers closer Kenley Jansen was lights out in his three innings, but with he and Kershaw getting no offensive support, the score remained 5-0 when Cubs closer Aroldis Chapman entered the game. On his third pitch, Chapman induced pinch-hitter Howie Kendrick to hit into an inning-ending, 4-6-3 double play.

With only three outs needed to send the Cubs to the World Series, the crowd of 42,386 inside Wrigley was in an uproar. Not to mention countless millions watching outside the park, in the bars and around the world.

Pinch-hitter Enrique Hernandez struck out swinging, pinch-hitter Carlos Ruiz walked and pinch-hitter Yasiel Puig grounded into a

120

short-to-second-to-first double play to end the Cubs' 5-0 win and bring 71 years of frustration to an end for the Cubs franchise and its long-suffering and loyal fan base.

The moment that millions of Cubs fans had waited for their entire lives finally occurred. The Chicago Cubs were National League champions… at last.

For the NLCS, Fowler batted .333, Rizzo .320, Baez .318 and Bryant .304, despite the fact that the Cubs were shut out in two of the six games. Russell and Rizzo had two homers each, Baez and Rizzo drove in five runs apiece, and Miguel Montero, Fowler and Russell each collected four RBI.

Four different Cubs pitchers – Hendricks, Lester, Montgomery and Chapman – were credited with wins, with Hendricks and Lester crafting ERAs of 0.71 and 1.38, respectively. Hendricks struck out 11, Lester nine, and Arrieta and Montgomery five each. Being named co-MVPs of the series were Baez and Lester.

Needless to say, the city of Chicago went nuts when the Cubs made history. And they were primed for a World Series-opening win at Progressive Field against the Cleveland Indians on Tuesday night, October 25. Cubs players and fans even had their hopes buoyed by the unexpected appearance of Kyle Schwarber, who had not played since tearing his anterior cruciate ligament and his lateral collateral ligament in an outfield collision during the third game of the season.

But Cleveland ace Corey Kluber had other thoughts in mind. His pitches were dancing all over the place during six innings of work. The hard-throwing right-hander established a World Series record by striking out eight batters in the first three innings, and he wound up with nine K's overall while allowing only four hits and no walks. ALCS MVP Andrew Miller escaped a couple of jams in his two innings of work and Cody Allen struck out three in the ninth to wrap up a 6-0 victory in Game 1.

Cubs starter Jon Lester was less sharp, giving up a pair of runs in the first inning and another in the fourth to take the loss. Left fielder Ben Zobrist was the only Cubs player to consistently swing the bat well, going 3-for-4, and Schwarber shook off the dust on his swing with a double off the right field wall in his second at-bat. Indians catcher Roberto Perez slugged a pair of homers and drove in four runs, while shortstop Francisco Lindor had three hits in four at-bats.

The start time for Game 2 in Cleveland was moved up an hour in hopes the game could be completed before predicted rains arrived. The strategy worked, as only the last couple of innings were wet. The Cubs' bats worked as well. They scored five runs in the first five innings, punched out nine hits overall and evened the series with a 5-1 triumph.

Cubs starter Jake Arrieta had some control issues, but was tossing a no-hitter with one out in the sixth inning when the Indians started getting to him. The right-hander gave up only one earned run in his 5.2 innings, allowing two hits and three walks while striking out six. Lefties Mike Montgomery (2 innings) and Chapman (1.1) held Cleveland scoreless the rest of the way.

The Cubs did not waste any time roughing up starting pitcher Trevor Bauer. Bryant singled to center with one out and Rizzo doubled him home in the first inning. Chicago added another run in the third with a two-out rally featuring a walk to Rizzo, a single by Zobrist and an RBI single by Schwarber.

Taking command of the game in the top of the fifth, the Cubs tallied three times. Rizzo walked for the second time and raced home on a triple by the red-hot Zobrist (5-for-8 through two games). Schwarber, whose single plated Zobrist, eventually trotted home on a bases-loaded walk to Russell. The Indians scored their only run in the sixth inning on a wild pitch by Arrieta.

Games 3 and 4 at Wrigley Field were more painful to watch for

Cubs fans than any games all season. The wind was howling out in Game 3, but the Cubs could do little more than hit ground balls and strike out. The wind was blowing in throughout Game 4, and the Cubs hit a bunch of fly balls that stayed in the yard. The bottom line? Cleveland executed and Chicago didn't. The Indians did all the little things right and the Cubs did all the little things wrong.

Chicago managed only five hits in Game 3, including two by right fielder Jorge Soler, against starter Josh Tomlin, winning pitcher Andrew Miller, setup man Bryan Shaw and closer Cody Allen. Cubs starter Kyle Hendricks did not allow a run, but was pulled following 4.1 innings after giving up six hits and two walks. Cleveland scored the only run of the game in the seventh inning on an RBI single by pinch-hitter Coco Crisp off losing pitcher Carl Edwards Jr.

In Game 4, Cubs bats were stifled yet again. They took a 1-0 lead in the first inning off Corey Kluber when Fowler led off with a double and Rizzo singled him home. But they were limited to one run the rest of the way – an eighth-inning homer by Fowler – in a 7-2 loss. Jason Heyward, Rizzo and Fowler combined for six hits, but the rest of the team managed only one between eight other batters.

Cleveland tallied in the second, third and sixth innings for a 4-1 advantage before second baseman Jason Kipnis applied the icing on the cake with a three-run homer into the right field bleachers in the seventh. Kluber was credited with the win after allowing one run over six innings. The Tribe now held a commanding three-games-to-one lead.

On a cool and breezy evening at Wrigley Field on October 30, the Cubs desperately needed a win to stay alive and the Indians sought the victory that would secure their first World Series title since 1948. The first five batters of Game 5 struck out, indicating what kind of game it was going to be.

Cleveland took a 1-0 lead in the second inning off Jon Lester when Jose Ramirez drove a two-out home run into the left field bleachers. Still trailing 1-0 heading into the bottom of the fourth, the Cubs rallied for three runs on a solo homer by Kris Bryant, an infield single by Addison Russell to score Anthony Rizzo, who had doubled, and a sacrifice fly by David Ross to plate Ben Zobrist, who had singled.

The Tribe cut their deficit in half in the sixth frame on an RBI single by Francisco Lindor, who was then caught trying to steal second by Ross. Now down 3-2, Cleveland put together a single, passed ball and hit batsman in the seventh inning, but was unable to score against Carl Edwards Jr. and Aroldis Chapman.

Chapman was making an extremely early entry into the game for a closer, but Cubs manager Joe Maddon wasn't going to bow out of the World Series without his best reliever on the hill. Chapman allowed a single and two stolen bases in the eighth, then retired the side in order in the ninth to preserve a 3-2 Cubs win.

For the game, Chicago struggled on offense once again, striking out 14 times against starter Trevor Bauer and three relievers. Russell had a pair of hits for the winners, who held Cleveland to six hits. Chapman struck out four and did not walk a batter in his 2.2 innings of work.

In Game 6 back at Progressive Field, the Cubs felt they needed to get on the board early if they were going to have a chance to win. That's just what they did. Batting in the third spot in the order, Kris Bryant belted a solo home run in the top of the first inning off Cleveland starter Josh Tomlin.

The right-hander would have gotten out of the inning without additional damage, but Addison Russell's fly ball dropped between two Indians outfielders – either of whom could have caught it – for a two-run double. The gift saw Anthony Rizzo and Ben Zobrist, both of whom had hit line drive singles, crossing the plate.

Still ahead 3-0 in the third inning, the Cubs loaded the bases

124

with one out for the 22-year-old Russell, who became the second youngest player in World Series history to hit a grand slam. (Mickey Mantle of the New York Yankees was 21 when he accomplished the feat in 1953.) Scoring on Russell's blast were Kyle Schwarber (walk), Rizzo (single) and Zobrist (single).

The Indians tried to creep back in it with single runs in the fourth and fifth innings, but the Cubs got those runs back in the ninth when Bryant singled for his fourth hit of the game and Rizzo smacked a long home run to right field for his third hit. For the game, the Cubs' No. 3 through 6 batters (Bryant, Rizzo, Zobrist and Russell) were a combined 11-for-19 with eight runs scored and nine RBI.

Winning pitcher Jake Arrieta gave up two runs on three hits and three walks while striking out nine over 5.2 innings. Mike Montgomery, Aroldis Chapman, Pedro Strop and Travis Wood recorded outs in relief during the 9-3 Cubs victory that evened the series at three games apiece.

The Cubs had now rallied from a three-games-to-one deficit, but how would they respond against the Indians ace, Corey Kluber, in their third consecutive elimination game? A crowd of 38,104 at Progressive Field – many wearing Cubs jerseys and hats – and a huge television audience around the world would find out, but not before witnessing an epic 4½-hour game.

The Cubs did not waste any time trying to take command. Leadoff man Dexter Fowler sent Kluber's fourth pitch sailing over the centerfield wall for a home run and a 1-0 lead. Designated hitter Kyle Schwarber then singled, shocking everybody in the park two outs later by stealing second. But he was stranded there when Ben Zobrist flied out.

Chicago starter Kyle Hendricks was reached for two singles in the bottom of the second, but he picked one base runner off first and got Rajai Davis to hit into a double play. The Indians then tied the game at

125

1-1 in the third when Coco Crisp doubled, advanced to third on Roberto Perez's sacrifice bunt and trotted home on a single by DH Carlos Santana.

The Cubs moved ahead 3-1 in the fourth inning. Bryant singled to left, Rizzo was hit by a pitch and Zobrist grounded into a fielder's choice, with Rizzo forced out at second. Russell then lifted a sacrifice fly to short center to score Bryant, and Zobrist raced home on a double by Willson Contreras.

After Hendricks retired the Indians in order in the fourth, Javy Baez led off the fifth with a home run to right-center. Later in the inning, Bryant walked and came all the way around to score on Rizzo's two-out single to right. The Cubs were in command with a 5-1 advantage, but Joe Maddon yanked Hendricks after he allowed a two-out walk in the fifth. Following an infield hit and a throwing error by newly-inserted catcher David Ross, Lester uncorked a wild pitch that was so wild, two runners crossed the plate to cut the lead to 5-3.

Ross got one of those runs back in the top of the sixth when he became the oldest player in World Series Game 7 history to homer. The blast off reliever Andrew Miller came in what would be Ross' final game of his career. Lester kept the Indians off the board in the sixth and seventh innings, but after a two-out infield single in the eighth, Maddon again made a pitching change.

The manager had been criticized by some for using his closer, Aroldis Chapman, in Game 6 with the Cubs ahead by five runs. Their critique seemed spot on when the left-hander immediately gave up an RBI double to Brandon Guyer and a two-run homer to Davis. Suddenly it was a brand new ballgame at 6-6. Crisp then singled to put the lead run on base, but Yan Gomes struck out to end the threat. Neither team was able to tally in the ninth inning.

The Indians and Cubs were headed to extra innings. But not quite yet. In what would later be viewed by many as a break needed far

126

more by the reeling Cubs who had blown a three-run lead than by the momentum-fueled Indians, a 17-minute rain delay intervened.

Cubs right fielder Jason Heyward, who had struggled offensively all season long and throughout most of the playoffs, quickly called an impromptu players-only meeting. During the brief session, he reminded his teammates how good they were, how all of them had contributed to the team's success and how they had everything they needed to win, as long as they believed in each other.

Having rebooted, the Cubs came out swinging in the top of the 10th. Schwarber led off with a single and pinch-runner Albert Almora shrewdly tagged up and advanced to second on a deep fly out by Bryant. After reliever Bryan Shaw intentionally walked Rizzo, Zobrist made him pay by lashing an RBI double to left field. Now perched on third base, Rizzo scampered home on a clutch single to left by Miguel Montero. Trevor Bauer came on to retire the next two Chicago batters, but the Cubs now led 8-6.

Being reminded once again that nothing comes easy, Cubs fans watched anxiously as Cleveland rallied in the bottom of the 10th with a two-out walk to Guyer and an RBI single by Davis against Carl Edwards Jr., who had replaced Chapman. Mike Montgomery then came on and got Michael Martinez to ground softly to Bryant at third base. Bryant's right foot gave out on the wet turf as he threw to first base, but Rizzo reached up and snagged the high throw for the final out.

The 8-7 victory in extra innings made the Cubs only the sixth team in baseball history to rally from a three games-to-one deficit to win the World Series. And, oh yeah, the Cubs ended the longest championship drought in American major sports history… 108 years.

For the game, Fowler and Schwarber had three hits each, Bryant scored two runs, and eight different batters had an RBI. Chapman was tagged with a blown save but was also credited with the win, while Montgomery earned the first save of his career. Davis drove in three runs for the Indians and Shaw was charged with the loss.

For the series, Schwarber hit .412 in 17 at-bats and walked three times; Rizzo batted .360 with team highs in hits (9), doubles (3) and runs (7); Bryant and Fowler hit two homers apiece; and Addison Russell collected a team-best nine RBI. Jake Arrieta won two games, posted a 2.38 ERA and struck out 15 batters; Kyle Hendricks crafted a 1.00 ERA over nine innings; and Jon Lester fanned a team-high 16.

Most deservedly, left fielder Ben Zobrist was named the 2016 World Series MVP for his consistently solid play throughout the series. The switch-hitter batted .357 with three extra-base hits, three walks and five runs scored.

A huge throng estimated at 5 million people attended the Cubs' victory parade on the streets of Chicago and the rally at Grant Park on Friday, November 4. It was labeled the seventh largest gathering in human history! Rizzo choked up while telling fans how much the retiring David Ross meant to him and the team, while Fowler called the crowd his family and Zobrist declared that his MVP award was really a team award… a team full of MVPs.

And very fittingly, the Cubs capped off this momentous occasion by leading the crowd in the singing of "Go Cubs Go." No song ever sounded sweeter. What a day and what a season! Cubs fans will never forget them.

* * *

During the 2016 season, I wondered if fervently hoping for the Cubs' first World Series title in my lifetime was an exercise in futility. Worse yet, I pondered whether I was setting myself up for yet another crushing disappointment. But what were my options?

Sure, I could have chosen to stay aloof and tried to watch the season unfold from an emotionally healthy distance. I could have continually told myself that the Cubs would eventually choke, and when they did, perhaps I'd be able to walk away unscarred.

But what if the Cubs actually did make it to the 2016 World Series? And what if they really did capture the Fall Classic for the first time since 1908? Would my elation have been tempered by the fact that I refused to become fully immersed in the charge for the prize? I had a feeling that might be the case, and I refused to let that happen.

'Tis better to have loved and lost than never to have loved at all. Alfred Lord Tennyson wasn't a Cubs fan, but I believe he was right. Yes, the pain of loss is severe, but the joy of love is stronger. And I don't think we're fully human if we don't experience both.

So, I took the risk of being called a fool for refusing to learn from the past. People reminded me that every single time I'd put my faith in the Chicago Cubs, the team ripped my heart out. They were right. They were absolutely, 100 percent correct.

But in 2016, I decided to ignore bad luck and curses. I threw caution to the wind that whipped in from Lake Michigan. I stepped on the cracks of the sidewalks outside Wrigley Field. I broke the rearview mirror that revealed a team gaining on the Cubs. I walked under the ladder the Cubs climbed to the Central Division championship. Heck, I even thought about getting a black cat and letting her saunter in front of the TV while I watched a game.

But I determined not to allow the seemingly endless setbacks of the past dampen the spirit of hope that indwells all of us Cubs fans. I knew I might be crying in my beer by myself in October. Then again, I realized I could possibly be toasting a title with the Wrigleyville faithful in November. Indeed, that's exactly what happened.

And it only took 108 years. Now, let's make sure we get that next championship before 2124, shall we?

Author's Notes:

Thank you very much for reading *Me and Ernie: Growing Up on Baseball in the Sixties and Finally Celebrating a Cubs World Series Title*. I have two favors to ask of you.

Please write a brief review on Amazon.com to let people know what you thought of this memoir, as that is a big help to readers in deciding whether to check it out.

Also, please send me an email at boyletimothy678@gmail.com so I can let you know about other books I've written and the ones on which I'm currently working, as well as any updates I might make to this book. Thanks, and Go Cubs!

Made in the USA
Monee, IL
20 December 2019